OUT TO LUNCH
Back in six hours

Tales of the unexpected, the unbelievable and the unforgivable

Stories about customers and customer service experiences

Published by the Institute of Customer Service
2 Castle Court St Peter's Street Colchester CO1 1EW
01206 571716
enquiries@icsmail.co.uk
instituteofcustomerservice.com
© Institute of Customer Service 2007

Cover and book design and typesetting by Wave Creative Communications
Cartoons by Anne-Marie Sonneveld
Printed and bound in Great Britain by CKN

A CIP catalogue record of this book is available from the British Library.

ISBN: 978-1-906080-01-3

The Institute of Customer Service has made every effort to trace and acknowledge
copyright holders. If any source has been overlooked, ICS would be pleased to redress
this for future editions.

Profits from the sale of this book will be shared equally by two charities that are
ICS Members: the RNIB and WWF-UK.

ICS Institute of Customer Service

Ted Johns has been Chairman of ICS since 2002 and a
Director since its incorporation in 1997. He is a prolific
author of books on ethical leadership, time management,
organisational change and customer care, and of articles
for such periodicals as *People Management*, *Management
Today*, *Marketing Insights*, *Employee Relations Review* and
the Institute's own *customerfirst*. He contributes a lively
column to each issue of *Customer Management* and its
online newsletter, and has also produced an
ICS Breakthrough Research Report which reviews the
research and other evidence underpinning the
ICS Model for World-Class Service.

Ted is regularly in demand as a keynote speaker for both
in-company and open-access conferences. According to
his customers, his presentations are thought-provoking,
challenging, provocative and highly entertaining.
He doesn't do boring.

This book is dedicated to all those who design, deliver and receive world-class customer service.

It is not dedicated to organisations that continue to assume they know what their customers want without actually asking them, that continue to think that their customer service is 'good enough' or those that rely on customer complaints as their sole source of performance feedback.

It is not dedicated to those customer service managers who seem to think that the way to achieve good customer service is to pay lip service to service excellence, demand the impossible, punish those who fail and only measure the easily measurable (call duration) rather than what's important (customer outcomes).

Contents

IAN SMITH
President, Institute of Customer Service

Regional Senior Vice President for the UK, Ireland, Israel and South Africa, Oracle Corporation UK Ltd

I count my role as President of the Institute of Customer Service as one of my proudest achievements. But it hardly seems possible that it is 10 years since I was first approached to become involved in what was then a revolutionary new organisation.

At that time, I was working as Director of Customer Service within BT's Consumer Division and experiencing at first-hand the pain some of my customers were undergoing – in more than one instance because a process was being followed correctly but the human element had been disregarded.

So it was both with interest and pleasure that I became involved in this new organisation. However, in the intervening 10 years, my interest has turned to sheer awe at the turnaround in the psyche of the British customer. For so many years, customers would mutter to each other but very infrequently make a direct complaint – although they would accept inappropriate behaviour from their supplier – because they felt they had no choice. And they were right – there were few choices available to them. The development of choices available to the customer was the catalyst which changed the concept and image of customer service forever.

One of the greatest impacts came from the increasing number of consumer programmes on television. Viewers learned that there were professional bodies to whom they could complain when they experienced an unsatisfactory purchase or service. They learned that the 'oxygen of publicity' was something that most companies feared and would avoid if possible – and that compensation could become an endgame in itself.

Most of all, though, as the years progressed customers learned that more and more choices were becoming available to them. New ways to shop, new ways to pay for their goods or services – and new ways to complain if either were unsatisfactory. They learned that they had the right to expect to be treated as individuals, with individual wants and needs, and if they didn't find that attitude with their current supplier, they learned they could simply move on to another one.

So, finally, more and more suppliers – retail, banks, hotels, holiday companies, you name it – learned that, to attract and retain customers, it was to their advantage to learn and implement the precepts of good customer service – to 'dazzle' their customers.

And the Institute of Customer Service has been right in the thick of that change: developing and encouraging customer service practitioners and corporations to take their place in a world in which customer needs are the drivers for the customer service experience. Long may it continue!

It is 9.15 am on a December Saturday in the late 1980s. We are standing outside the newly-refurbished Woolworths store in North Street, Chichester. It has just re-opened after a massive refit. Gone is the original red and gold fascia, the old-fashioned lettering, the wooden counters and the sawdust floors, to be replaced by a white and grey colour scheme, set off by a multi-coloured pick 'n' mix section right in the middle of the ground floor, and a focus on six product groups. Fortunately one of the six product groups permits the sale of Christmas decorations because that is the central purpose of our hero's mission today.

Already people are scurrying into and out of Woolworths. They constitute the normal detritus of a Saturday – large young ladies in fluorescent shell-suits (acceptable attire for the 1980s), parents with elaborate child-buggies built like minefield-clearance vehicles, children with pocket-money to spend at the pick 'n' mix counter and early-morning pensioners who simply want to find somewhere warm.

But who is this, hovering uncertainly in the outfield? He is not your average Woolworths' customer because he is witty (you will have to take my word for this, since he has yet to speak), urbane, sophisticated, elegant and sharply groomed. Very unusually for a Saturday morning in Chichester, he is wearing a collar and tie, for this is simply part of what he calls 'style'.

Can this person be the very author of the honeyed words dripping off the page presently in your hands? Yes, reader, he can and he is.

He is here on a mission to purchase an eight-foot plastic Christmas tree. This is not, he would hasten to say, a mission of his own. Indeed, if prompted, he would rapidly distance himself from the task to which ostensibly he is committed because this is a mission communicated to him by his then wife. It is therefore, properly speaking, someone else's mission and he is simply doing what he is told.

He has risen early to attack the

Christmas tree display in Woolworths before the Saturday panic begins. He reasons that if he makes his purchase before 10 am, there is a good chance that nobody he knows will see him entering the store and nobody will see him walking away with an eight-foot plastic monstrosity in his arms. Frankly, he does not believe there is much social credit to be gained by shopping at Woolworths. He regards this adventure as equal in attractiveness to the prospect of having an abscess removed without the benefit of anaesthetic. By getting it over early he has confronted his pain at the start of the day and so the rest of Saturday will be uphill, particularly if *Doctor Who* is on television later.

Standing unobtrusively under the balcony of the city's Town Hall, opposite Woolworths, our hero carefully surveys the street scene. Confident that there is nobody he recognises and, more importantly, nobody who recognises him, he finally plucks up courage and walks stealthily into the store. He is immediately assailed by a familiar smell – a combination of boiled sweets, chocolate, plastic, vinyl, household cleansers, disinfectant and sweaty armpits. It is a heady mixture and takes him back nostalgically to his childhood Woolworths, where each counter had its own till, staff had to calculate your change in their heads and the phrase 'checkout operator' had yet to be invented.

Pinching himself in order to return to the present, our hero inspects the racks of artificial Christmas trees. Shock, horror: *there is no eight-foot tree*. To be truthful, there is one, but it is out of reach on a wall display.

Pausing momentarily to reflect on the pointlessness of placing trees where customers can't get at them, he briefly considers his options. He could walk out and drive to Bognor Regis in the hope that there are eight-foot trees there. He could purchase a six-foot tree and seek to persuade his wife that this would be more suitable or even persuade her that it will shortly grow into an eight-foot tree. He could investigate alternative sources of supply, such as local garden centres.

None of these courses of action has anything to commend them. All of them involve work and unpleasant work at that. All of them will take up time that could be better spent doing something else. All of them involve expense. Even the attempt to persuade his wife of the merits of a six-foot tree could prove costly, in ways which cannot be discussed in a book intended for family consumption. All of them, in short, are emotionally distressing to someone who simply wants to get this over with.

So there's nothing for it. He must find someone who works in Woolworths and ask them either to take down the eight-foot tree from the wall display or to find an eight-foot tree in their stockroom. This is not a trivial decision, for our hero is a man and he is not used to asking for information. He will travel miles down the wrong roads to avoid consulting maps. Nor is he used to complaining or admitting in any way that he is not totally in command of the situation. Like most men, he will normally push his wife forward whenever questions have to be asked, goods have to be returned or complaints have to be complained.

Fortunately he sees three young Woolworths employees striding purposefully in his direction. They have no intention of speaking to him or indeed to any other customer – for they are on their way to the staff rest area for a well-deserved cup of coffee. After all it is 9.15 am and they've been working solidly for a quarter of an hour and it is the 1980s when speaking to customers was not a requirement in anyone's job description.

Our hero bravely plants himself in their path and accosts them. They are forced to stop because he is directly in their way and he thinks it unlikely that they will deliberately push him to the ground.

He asks them, with appropriate signals and body language, if they will be so kind as to bring down the eight-foot tree on the wall or find an eight-foot tree from the stockroom. He is not threatening, aggressive or violent – he knows his place in the scheme of things – and indeed his voice has a somewhat beseeching quality about it. Much good may it do him.

The three look at each other, each hoping that this impossible and unreasonable assignment will not be dumped on them. In the end, the young lady (the only one who is a permanent member of staff, it turns out, since the other two are 'Saturday people' – a phrase which suggests that they don't exist on any other days of the week) cracks and she tells one of the Saturday people to have a look in the stockroom. She is clearly the boss and, equally clearly, she has learned the science of delegating or, more precisely, the art of shifting unpleasant work to others.

None of the three has spoken a word to our hero. As they disappear into the distance he is left to wonder whether any will ever return. After all, the one who has left for the stockroom had not been instructed to report back. Possibly it won't occur to him to do so, young people being somewhat lacking in initiative and gumption these days (or, at least, so thinks our hero). The other two members of the trio have gone altogether, presumably having dismissed the problem of the eight-foot artificial Christmas tree from their effervescent minds. They have more important things to think about, like where they will be going that night, who they will be going with and what they might do when they get there. As we have already seen, possession of any social skills is not a requirement for job applicants in the world of retailing throughout the late 1980s.

After a few moments the stockroom-searcher comes back. He is mildly triumphant because, he believes, he has solved the customer's problem and has used his creative powers at the same time. He has exercised what we would nowadays call 'empowerment' and he has 'gone the extra mile'. Clearly he expects that his initiative will be rewarded and recognised with a display of heartfelt gratitude.

"Sorry guv," he begins. This is not a good start. 'Guv' is a mode of address which our hero finds unattractive, and he does not respond enthusiastically or positively. 'Guv' is marginally preferable to 'squire' or 'boss' or 'captain', but that does not make it endearing. It is a lot better than 'darling'. However, our hero is prepared to let all this pass because he has his eye fixed on the potential accomplishment of his mission which is, if you haven't lost the will to live, to return home with an eight-foot artificial Christmas tree. Nothing must be allowed to get in the way of this supreme objective.

"Sorry guv," claims our young helper. "We don't have any more eight-foot Christmas trees but I've found two four-foot ones – will they do?"

We will draw a veil over our hero's response which even now, 20 years later, causes him to cringe with embarrassment. Surely he could not have been so crudely aggressive towards another human being – one, moreover, who had simply done his best, even if his best was nowhere, and I do mean *nowhere*, like good enough. Let's just say that our Woolworths friend received some feedback and personal advice of an unusually direct and unequivocal kind, and it did not make his day. It may have even spoiled his evening. The advice included some guidance about what to do with one or both of the four-foot trees. Acting on this advice would have proved very painful.

It was largely this experience, plus a few other comparable ones, which prompted our hero to begin thinking and writing about customer service. Such is the significance of seemingly trivial encounters. But what we need to think about is what this story tells us about customer service then and now.

First, in those days customer service was almost universally perceived to be something solely concerned with putting things right after they had gone wrong.

If it was good, it was remedial, reactive and responsive – and people expected no more from it. Anyone defining customer service would have done so exclusively in terms of problem-solving, service recovery and service restitution (or compensation). The customer service department was a type of corporate back-stop – there to mop up the awful consequences of failure somewhere else in the product/service delivery system.

This means that the service function was starved of resources – money, talent, facilities and time. Nobody who was ambitious wanted to work in the customer services department since it was a backwater for no-hopers, losers and failures.

It didn't seem to occur to anyone that actually customer service is precisely the sort of role where damage on an unprecedented scale can be inflicted – initially on customers but subsequently, of course, on the prosperity and very survival of the business. Customers who are wounded as a result of the service they receive will take their business elsewhere and encourage all their friends and relatives to do the same. They in turn encourage all their friends and relatives to defect and so the blood-letting continues, through an endless succession of reflecting mirrors.

Most larger businesses in the 1980s didn't believe that interaction with people was seen by customers as important. Interestingly, in the 1980s, when Woolworths went through a major corporate restructuring leading to their new focus on only six product groups, they spent many millions of pounds on their stores – *but spent virtually nothing on their people*. This meant that when a Woolworths re-opened after its gut-and-refit exercise, the people working there behaved exactly as they had behaved before, i.e. they devoted more attention to talking to each other than to any customers who might accidentally pass through their field of vision. Customers, always sensitive to ambience and atmosphere rather than technology and trappings, came to believe that in essence nothing had changed at all.

This has never been the mistake that small businesses have made because they have always realised – intuitively rather than scientifically – that their prosperity depends on creating positive relationships with their customers.

Proper relationships with customers, moreover, in turn depend on the quality of the extent to which each is made to feel important, wanted and valued, and the willingness of the organisation to cater for the customer's individual needs. No wonder restaurants flourish when they have a pivotal head waiter who understands the significance of these emotional dynamics. Clearly the food has to be good, the seats comfortable, the wine-list impressive – but plenty of restaurants have failed, despite offering good food, comfortable seats and an impressive wine-list, simply because their people skills have been deficient.

The next point to consider is that in the companies of yesteryear, staff were neither recruited, selected, trained or rewarded for the types of customer service capabilities that gradually customers were coming to demand. Certainly these organisations did not measure their service reputations or, if they did, such measures were frequently overridden by what were considered to be far more important indices of effectiveness like short-term profitability and cost control. True, most employers didn't like it if their employees were blatantly rude but the concept of 'service excellence' was something that was quite unknown.

Yet another consideration must remain the fact that until the 1990s many organisations did not have to compete for customers at all, either because they were monopolies or because the demand for their products and services exceeded supply to the extent that the suppliers could afford to be autocratic, paternalistic, inflexible and arrogant.

Some of you reading this book may even be able to remember the days when there were only the 'Big Five' banks on the high street – they all offered the same interest rates (moving them in unison as they responded to changes in bank rate). The idea of transferring your account to another bank was unheard of, just as it was unheard of for any bank employee to leave to work for a 'competitor' bank. If you wanted a mortgage you didn't go to your bank – because of some clever demarcation barriers banks didn't do mortgages and building societies didn't do overdrafts but you had to be interviewed by the building society with which you had already opened a savings account.

Even if you had a savings account, it was by no means guaranteed that your mortgage application would be successful, but what was certain was that other building societies wouldn't even give you the time of day. In any case, all the building societies charged the same rate of interest, all applied the same multiples to the husband's earnings and all of them specified the same terms and conditions.

Nobody complained about any of this. It was 'the system'. Everyone had lived with it for a long time. The building societies loved it (people with power generally do love any 'system' that preserves the status quo). Couples knew they had to be married even to qualify for a mortgage, the husband was automatically viewed as the sole or principal breadwinner. We couldn't imagine any other kind of existence.

It all seems unbelievable today when we have banks competing for our business (rather than the other way round), building societies turning themselves into banks, new banks and foreign banks appearing on our radar, lenders paying no attention to whether mortgagees are married but instead offering multiples of up to six times the salaries of the putative property purchasers, with few questions asked.

Product/service suppliers that are monopolies find it more difficult to provide a level of customer service that could be described as 'world-class', even when they actively seek to do so. Why might this be? Well, whether you like it or not, you have to 'buy' local government services from your local authority, water from your water utility, passports from the Passport Agency, roads from the Department of Transport. Some of these 'businesses' can easily fall into the trap of thinking that because you are, as it were, a tied customer then it's your job to fit round their processes and systems. They may even laugh at the possibility that they could change their processes and systems to fit round the customer. What an absurd concept!

So it's not surprising if the relationship between us and, say, our local planning department becomes more like a servant/master relationship than a relationship based on consenting equals, especially if we are the supplicants seeking some form of publicly-sanctioned approval like planning permission. We fill in the forms as conscientiously, accurately, diligently and legibly as possible – after all, we don't want to do anything that gives them an excuse to send the forms back or become irritated with us. If it's a passport renewal or application, we have to make sure our signature doesn't encroach on the borders of the box in which the signature has to be written. We've only ourselves to blame if we muck that up because we've been supplied with blank boxes so that we can practise what we have to do. Similarly, our passport photographs must be just so – not too high or too low, not too dark or too light, not too close or too distant.

And we mustn't look too cheerful, either, otherwise some passport official in one of the more distant parts of the globe may run away with the idea that we are happy to be British.

Similarly, it's interesting how people who can be very aggressive and demanding customers in most fields of endeavour suddenly become docile and subservient when receiving hospital or medical treatment. It's as if we fear we might be 'accidentally' dropped down the waiting list if we prove truculent or our injections could be administered that little bit more ruthlessly if we are classified as a troublemaker.

Once people begin to think they are the dominant partner in a relationship it's not unusual for them to become inflexible, demanding and unyielding. When they do relax 'the rules' in some minor way, we are pathetically grateful and we promise faithfully not to spoil their lives again. We may even mean it. In this way – by the random delivery of miniscule concessions and the implied threat of their withdrawal – the power of the dominant partner is reinforced.

Does any of the above ring bells with you? To be even more pointed, does it remind you of your school days at all, when you were but a humble novice, surrounded by the tangible evidence of arbitrary adult authority? Is that the kind of relationship that you'd like to have with the people who supply customer service to you? No, of course it isn't. Thankfully, for the most part, such relationships have disappeared off the face of our society – maybe, argue some, it's even gone too far the other way though we'll come to that in a minute.

Twenty years ago, customers themselves were different people. As recently as 10 years ago, customers were more docile, more tolerant, more philosophical, more grateful. It was relatively rare for customers to be driven beyond endurance – even though that is precisely what happened when our hero (already in a negative frame of mind, it has to be said, at the prospect of purchasing an artificial Christmas tree) was confronted by a mixture of indifference and misguided assistance. If customers didn't complain or didn't do so in large numbers, then no wonder many organisations believed that their service performance was impeccable – especially if their only measure of service performance was the number of complaints they received.

What has changed?

Well, we have to admit that for some organisations not much has changed at all. There are still those who regard customer service as a low priority affair and who still treat customers as if they were an unpleasant irritant, causing mayhem to the tidy and elegant landscape of corporate harmony and the calm, unruffled, well-ordered patterns of organisational routine.

There are still organisations that haven't switched themselves on to the real world of the 21st century, where customers are powerful and promiscuous (not in the sexual sense, but that they can shift their business and their 'loyalty' easily from one service supplier to another and not feel even a slight twinge of guilt). These organisations have been forced to function competitively but are reluctant to undergo the type of transformation which the new world should entail. Instead, they try to keep their customers at arm's length. They deliberately engage in 'confusion marketing' by creating a multiplicity of pricing packages that virtually prevent the customer from making intelligent, informed choices They design and operate automated telephone systems that give customers the type of runaround which causes them ultimately to admit defeat. They fail to answer correspondence or emails, refuse to give any of their staff the authority to use their initiative when resolving customer problems and justify their 'rules' by claiming that they are merely implementing 'the law' and/or the disciplines imposed upon them by interfering regulators.

There are still people in directly customer-facing roles who shouldn't be there and who probably shouldn't be interacting with people at all. This can happen because some organisations regard all their people – especially in lower level positions – as virtually interchangeable. You can be a shelf-stacker one day, a bakery assistant the next and a checkout operator on the third. No wonder some find themselves dealing with customers when that's something they never wanted to do either because they don't have the skills for it or because they'd simply rather be doing something else.

And who suffers from this sorry mismatch? Well, everyone does: people who are unhappy in their jobs, customers who are unhappy with the way they are treated and organisations that are unhappy with the constant flow of customer complaints, high labour turnover and customer defections. Ironically, then, organisations don't like what's happening but don't think through the causes and accept their own responsibility for the outcomes. It's much more likely that they blame everyone but themselves – they blame their customers for being so fickle and irresponsible as to go somewhere else, they blame their employees for behaving so badly or incompetently and then they blame their employees again for leaving altogether. Lots of blame by lots of people, all in denial, all seeing the specks in other people's eyes but not the beams in their own. Brilliant.

There are still organisations that seek to compete solely on the basis of price and cost. These organisations (and you know who they are) pretend that they can't afford to supply superior service on the (false) grounds that to do so would add hugely to their costs while ignoring the reality that, in fact, excellent service is the cheapest possible option for a company to pursue. That's because if you get it right first time all the time (and there's no reason why you shouldn't), you don't have to spend anything on putting right what has gone wrong. However, there will always be some businesses that will compete on price and there will always be a minority who will manage to make reasonable profits from doing so. The majority will not because competing on price means that margins (profits) are constantly being squeezed; until only the largest players can benefit from the economies of scale that permit their operations to be undertaken at the lowest competitive cost. Competing by price, therefore, is ultimately unrewarding (except, as I say, for the favoured few) – far better to compete on the basis of perceived *value*.

If this tirade has depressed you then let's start to think positive for a change. Some may argue that nothing has changed but the majority of us believe that everything has changed.

- In many fields of endeavour, where once there was monopoly (a single supplier) or oligopoly (a small group of similar suppliers), there is now competition red in tooth and claw. Competition is invariably advantageous for customers because it means that organisations must fight for our business instead of taking it for granted; this in turn means that we benefit from lower prices, more innovative products and services – and better customer service (even if, sometimes, it seems a long time coming)

- Because existing product/service suppliers were often poor at supplying service, while simultaneously charging exorbitant prices for it, new entrants have seized the opportunities presented in an 'open skies' marketplace. So we now have, in banking, new entrants like First Direct (actually not so new now as it first hit the streets in 1994) that offer a standard of customer contact, a friendliness of customer relationships and a responsiveness to customer requirements that is virtually unequalled anywhere

- Successive Governments have seen both the economic and political benefits to be gained from encouraging competition in the private sector and service excellence in the public sector, even though in practice politicians seem torn between the need to encourage competition on the one hand and the desire to retain controls over unbridled competition on the other. Thus, the purpose of the Competition Commission is essentially to ensure that no single company obtains too much ascendancy in its marketplace at the expense of its competitors and its customers. Already Tesco now secures £1 for every £7 spent by consumers in the UK which must mean that it is dangerously close to the point at which further expansion in the UK will be prevented – and it is perhaps for this reason that Tesco must now concentrate more of its strategic expansion overseas

- Above all, of course, we customers are no longer the cowed, submissive lot that we were 20 or 30 years ago. We're different. We're more prepared to complain, we're more aware of our 'rights' (and if we don't have a legal 'right' to reinforce what we want, we're quite prepared to pretend that we have or invent some moral 'right' instead), we're more aggressive (both verbally and, in some instances, physically) and more litigious. We're a lot more promiscuous, too

- Most customers now enjoy a number of alternative ways through which they can do business. At one time, if we wanted to talk to our bank we had to phone and/or make an appointment with the manager or one of his (managers were always male) acolytes. Today, we can manage our bank accounts online and shift from one bank to another without talking to anyone or having to defend ourselves. We scarcely ever need to write a cheque and the cheque as a means of transferring money from one place to another is on the way out – even money itself is less useful. The growing impersonality of our connections with 'our' bank is indeed one of the reasons why we are becoming more relaxed about changing banks, simply because there is no 'relationship' between us and the bank manager that we need feel guilty about if we up sticks and go elsewhere

- Another thing about customers is that many of us have been around a lot more and we've experienced or heard and read about the type of customer service that is routinely delivered by Disney, Singapore Airlines and Shangri-La Hotels. We buy leisure clothes from Lands End, we have a savings account with Nationwide, we get our lunchtime sandwiches and latte from Pret A Manger. We know what it is to ring our bank if it's First Direct and speak to a human being who shows a genuine interest in resolving our problem or in satisfying our needs. We have a better understanding about what can be done when organisations are focused on service excellence as their key competitive differentiator and that has made us think three things:

1. **We are less likely to accept statements (aka 'excuses') that some desired level of service responsiveness is 'impossible' or 'can't be done'** because we already have the evidence in front of our eyes that the 'impossible' is being achieved somewhere else. 'If they can do it, why can't you?' seems to me to be a very relevant, legitimate and appropriate question to put to some of the organisations that we have to deal with

2. **We are now prone to be dissatisfied with a level of customer service that we once tolerated or took for granted.** It may have been 'good enough' in the past but now it isn't

3. **We are less trusting and therefore more challenging, more cynical and more critical.** In some respects, I concede, this is an unhealthy development – not every organisation is trying to rip us off – but it is one that is understandable

- We now live in a globalised world. Not only does that mean we've got out a lot more but it also means that organisations originating from other parts of the world have been able to invade our economy and show us what can be done. Toyota and BMW have shown us how to make cars that perform, Canon has shown us how to make photocopiers that work and Japanese companies generally have shown us how to get the best out of people. Of course, globalisation is not a universal good and undoubtedly it has caused some painful times for the UK economy, especially when some businesses have chosen to take some of their back-office functions and even their front-office customer-contact activities to other parts of the world (especially India) where labour and infrastructure costs are currently lower. Even here, however, the backlash from customers – irritated beyond belief by having to converse with customer service people whose ability to understand idiomatic English is marginal at best – has prompted many of these otherwise cost-driven organisations to think again. They must train their local staff more efficiently or restrict them to support roles that don't require direct contact with the customer or they must bring their customer service back into the UK. Whichever way, this is globalisation in action – jobs can move across national borders but only if customers themselves permit it.

Into this shifting and confusing scenery came the Institute of Customer Service in 1997. From the start we set about the business of making a difference:

- for the people who directly deliver service to customers

- for the experience of customers

- for the organisations that became our members (either because they knew their service performance needed drastic attention or because they wanted to stay ahead of the game)

- for the economy as a whole.

We were created to help build a proper sense of pride, self-esteem, dignity and self-worth among those who supply service to customers. Above all, we wanted (and still want) to create a culture of **professionalism** among those working in any activity that involves direct contact with customers, whether they are actually called 'customers' or 'clients', 'users', 'patients', 'passengers' or anything else. What matters is not what the recipients of customer service are called but that, whoever they are, they are are treated with respect, with courtesy, with consideration for their needs and with care for their feelings.

And it rapidly became apparent to us that if customers are to be treated respectfully, courteously, considerately and sensitively, then the people who do the treating should themselves be treated with respect, courtesy, consideration and sensitivity. This probably seems self-evident to you (I certainly hope it does) but I'm afraid it wasn't self-evident when ICS began its journey and it still isn't self-evident in some enterprises where customer-facing people continue to be expected to treat the customer like gold while they themselves are treated like dirt.

If our first concern was the **professionalism** of those at the sharp end of customer service, our second and parallel concern was with the **performance** of the organisations – in any sector – that create the strategies, the processes, the systems and the infrastructure that underpins the practice of customer service. Thus our mission (what we do) quickly translates itself into this simple message: **We lead customer service performance and professionalism**.

Throughout our development – during a period which has seen, and continues to see, a massive growth in concern about service excellence on the part of organisations and a massive escalation in power on the part of customers – we have worked within a number of assumptions that form the backbone of our programme:

- **Service excellence is primarily dependent on the people through whom customer service is delivered**

- **Technology is part of the service infrastructure, so efficient IT is an enabler and not normally a source in itself of customer 'delight'. This doesn't mean that technology isn't important but simply that it has to be kept in its place**

- **Customer service is an enormously significant opportunity for competitive and reputational advantage for all organisations, irrespective of sector**

Stories about customers and customer service experiences

- **A positive reputation for customer service encourages customers to become 'active promoters', freely recommending the organisation to their friends, relatives, colleagues and neighbours – to the point where the organisation need not advertise at all because its customers act as its unpaid marketing department**

- **The goal is not to produce customer 'satisfaction' but to create customer 'delight' through customer experiences that are an integrated mixture of the physical and the emotional.**

We are not complacent – we know we have come a long way but we also know we have a long way to go. We are even more well aware that our journey will never be finished because as organisations improve their customer service, so we customers continue to demand more from the organisational services we receive.

Some parts of this book should make you weep, other parts should make you smile, and still others may make the hairs on the back of your neck tingle with pleasure and excitement. I hope that many parts will remind you of your own customer service experiences – perhaps because you provide a service yourself to your customers and more or less simultaneously receive customer service from others. I hope, too, that you don't recognise yourself when reading about some of the dismal service scenarios that are scattered throughout these pages.

**TED JOHNS
Chairman
Institute of Customer Service
October 2007**

I would welcome stories from your own organisations, your own customer experiences or your own experiences with customers, for future editions of this book. Please send them to me at ted.johns@icsmail.co.uk and at the same time let me know whether you would like to be identified as the contributor. Clearly, for reasons I hope will be obvious, we have the right to edit your material but we will do our best to retain its original flavour.

Reputation, Reputation, Reputation

"Organisations live or die by their reputations.

Reputations can be for excellent service, reliable products, ethical policies or size and speed of growth, for example.

Positive reputations can confer powerful competitive advantage and also help organisations to attract better staff, suppliers and customers, and apply higher margins to their business."

Professor Robert Johnston, *Service Excellence=Reputation=Profit*

Institute of Customer Service, 2001

In the pages that follow you are going to read stories about customer service, about customers, about the people who deliver customer service and about the organisations that determine what level of customer service they deliver.

Sometimes we name names, because we think they deserve it and sometimes we don't, because we think that they should get a second chance.

Several stories come from the results of our Service Reputations Survey in which we asked a nationwide sample of respondents, using a scale between 'outstanding' and 'dreadful' to appraise their experiences of customer service within 31 sectors, embracing supermarkets, travel/transport, leisure/ entertainment, utilities, financial services, etc. We also invited them to tell us about their specific 'outstanding' and 'dreadful' service experiences, preferably from named organisations.

In some respects the results were unsurprising. We discovered that estate agents are not widely admired or respected, for example. We learned that many customers have had 'outstanding' experiences at the hands of such companies as the Nationwide Building Society, the John Lewis Partnership, Pret A Manger, First Direct and Lakeland. Nothing new there.

Elsewhere our survey produced some startling revelations and some incredibly rich material. Yet I feel obliged to insert a note of caution. Our sample was self-selected and almost certainly included a majority of people who had strong feelings about customer service, generally because their psychic equilibrium had been permanently damaged as a result of single traumatising service encounters with, say, a particularly obstreperous member of the security team at Heathrow airport.

Also, the stories that people tell about their service experiences have almost certainly become distorted with the re-telling. They may have been true at one time but in the repeated versions the memory inevitably begins to play tricks. It's likely that parts of the recollected experience will have been forgotten, other parts magnified and 'facts' mucked about with. Elements of an incident that reflect badly on the narrator (for example, some initial rudeness that could have partially justified an aggressive reaction) may have been quietly ignored. And, like plastic surgery, some wishful thinking has been allowed to intervene.

We recognise, too, that from an organisation's point of view, its service reputation may not be the same as its delivered service quality. Reputation, while crucially important and worth enhancing at almost any cost, is dependent on people's perceptions of past events which in turn may have been overly influenced by a small number of high-profile *causes célèbres*.

In practice, none of this matters. What does matter is that customer stories – however imperfectly disseminated – help to mould the reputation of the business which lies at the centre of each customer's experiences. If distortions intrude, this simply means that sometimes the organisation benefits from a partially-undeserved collection of bouquets or can suffer from an equally unwarranted bucket of brickbats. That's life and nobody ever said that life is fair (or if they did, then they were fools).

What matters, too, is reputation itself. Brands are about reputation and we must never forget that ultimately the reputation of the business, and the strength of its brands, depend on the decisions of the customer. Nothing else. I've often heard marketing people talk as if they 'own' the brands they represent, but they don't. Ask Gerald Ratner.

Brand value can mean the opportunity to sustain market share, to generate extra profitability and to survive in the long term when others are struggling to cope with consumer resistance and apathy.

When all our cautious caveats have been inserted and then trodden on, what remains? Well, the first thing that amazed me from our Service Reputations Survey was how some of our respondents interpreted the word 'outstanding' when they told us about their exceptional service experiences. For me, and I suspect most of you reading this book, 'outstanding' service is something that makes you tingle inside, something almost orgasmic, something amazingly memorable, something that makes you say "Wow!" either to yourself or to others.

Orgasmic service experiences in action

A friend stays at the Hilton Hotel in the Maldives for a holiday that includes his birthday. On the day, he proudly displays his birthday cards around the bedroom occupied by himself and his wife.

They return to their room after dinner in the evening to find the words 'HAPPY BIRTHDAY STUART' marked out in rose petals across the bed. **Wow!**

An insurance company allows its contact centre staff to spend up to £25 each month on creating 'customer delight' experiences for callers.

A policyholder phones to ask for a replacement policy renewal form because her little girl has crayoned over the original to the point where it is now illegible.

The contact-centre agent sends a replacement form, plus an A4 drawing pad and a box of coloured crayons. **Wow!**

For a special minority of people, however, 'outstanding' service occurs when a supplier does what it should be doing in the ordinary course of business. One of our informants told us that he regularly secured 'outstanding' service from Barclaycard because: "They have always transferred my money when requested", as though this were some kind of exceptional, astonishing and amazing event. Another nominated one of the big banks because: "Throughout my life the bank has always accommodated my demands and done what I have requested. A recent example was when I wished to bank a cheque". Perhaps the ability to bank a cheque successfully in a bank branch is indeed something to shout about. If so, things are worse than we thought.

"I don't believe it" - what they do to us

Scanning the columns of an Indian news magazine, as you do, I've come across a brilliant service innovation. Frankly, I'm surprised it hasn't been copied over here – though perhaps it has, without me knowing it.

In the part of India covered by the Western Railway Company, customers have been asking for an extra train in the evening between Dahanu and Virar. This problem has now been solved.

> *"Of course, we would ideally like to run an extra train between Dahanu and Virar,"* a spokesman for the Western Railway told reporters, *"but we don't have any spare locomotives at the moment. However, our customers kept telling us that they wanted an extra train, and we always listen to our customers, so we decided to put an extra service in the new timetable, leaving Dahanu at 19.50 and arriving at Virar at 21.00. Okay, it only runs on paper for now, but isn't that better than nothing? Next year we're hoping to buy a new train and then perhaps it will run in reality too".*

Ashok Churi, for one, of the Indian Railways Luggage Pass and Passengers' Association, is not satisfied.

> *"The Western Railway is cheating passengers,"* he has said, *"and it's wasting their time. Yesterday there were over a thousand passengers at Dahanu station waiting to board the 19.50, but no train came. Western Railways' advertising slogan is 'You Will Be Chuffed'. But I think it should be, 'Our Company Has Gone Off The Rails'".*

Well, exactly. Leaving aside the doubtful provenance of the strapline, 'You Will Be Chuffed', you have to wonder at the cheek of a business which evidently believes that putting an invisible train on its timetable is better than running no train at all. Wait a minute, though. The beauty of providing a service that exists solely on paper is that nothing can go wrong with it. If it's a train, it's always beautiful, all the toilets are immaculate, all the passengers well-behaved, its punctuality record is 100%.

Stories about customers and customer service experiences

And if the Western Railway can get away with this kind of thing, why don't we learn a few lessons from them and try the same approach here? For example:

- Companies could publicise customer helpline phone numbers but leave them unstaffed so that the phone rings but nobody answers. Incoming emails could disappear into what I call 'the black hole of eternal space'

- Alternatively, an automated response requires the customer to "leave a message" as "all our agents are busy at present", although "your call is valuable to us"

- When a telephone is finally answered, a solution – or compensation, or restitution, or an answer – could be promised, but the matter would immediately be forgotten. Sometimes this 'forgetting' may be ceremonially symbolised by the tearing up of the Post-it Note upon which the customer's details have been recorded

- All incoming letters or emails from customers could be either binned or deleted, whichever is technologically appropriate, though a 'holding' letter or message may be sent, saying that whatever you were writing about will be urgently investigated

- If there is no system for accepting complaints, then the organisation will have zero complaints. It can then boast about its excellent levels of customer satisfaction. Any complaint that gets through by mistake can be reclassified as a customer query

- Products and services can be promoted without any tangible change in the organisation's existing product/service offering. If anyone shows interest in these 'new' products or services, they can be told that they are merely an early expression of the company's strategic aspirations, like the 'concept cars' shown in Geneva. If the time comes when these products or services are offered in the flesh, as it were, then of course you will be the first to be told.

Fortunately, of course, none of the above has ever been practised in the customer service environment of this country and let's hope they never are.

If train services are advertised but don't exist, then the worlds of fantasy and reality are all mixed up together. No different, though, from the rhetoric about customer commitment and service excellence produced by some organisations that delude themselves about how good they are, how focused they are and how much their customers must love them because, look, they keep coming back for more.

Like wolves, we can cry out for a refreshing dose of truth and honesty, but sometimes we are baying for the moon. The Western Railway Company has it right after all: at least when it created a mythical train, it made no secret about the fact that it was doing so.

A customer for a well-known telecoms business (we won't name it, but you can take your pick) tells of what happened after the company's fourth failure to turn up as promised to fix his phone line. His American wife - accustomed to 'service with a smile' - called the firm's customer services department, but they couldn't help. Demanding to speak with someone senior, she was told: "You can ask to speak to someone else if you like but here the higher up they are, the less they know".

Caller: "I'd like to speak to the Health and Safety Manager, please."

Post Office employee: "I'm afraid that's not possible. He's not customer-facing."

Extract from telephone conversation with the Post Office Customer Care Department quoted in Private Eye

The Morgan Guaranty Trust Company in New York once ordered staff to stop saying 'Hello' to each other, claiming that such a friendly greeting is "out of place in the world of business".

Have you ever tried to return a faulty product to [well-known electrical appliance shop]? Not one you've just decided you don't like but one which is broken? I complained to Trading Standards about a £150 faulty phone system which took me one and a half hours to get my money back. The TSO said: "Well, you know where you went wrong, don't you? You went in there. You won't catch one of us shopping in there. Next time, remember, bargepole".

Respondent to the ICS Service Reputations Survey, 2003-05

The good news for the customer was that his car insurance renewal was a walkover. They had his card details, payment would be automatic, no worries.

Five days later, a letter: "Thank you for contacting us to confirm you do not wish to renew your policy."

So our man has been driving round illegally for five days.

To the phone: "Oh, yes, it says here we don't have your card details and we wrote to let you know."

"But the letter says nothing about a card, it says the policy's not renewed."

"Yes, well, we don't have a letter which mentions card details, so we sent the nearest letter we had."

Terry Wogan's column, Sunday Telegraph, 25 October 2006

YES MADAM, I'VE TAKEN DOWN YOUR DETAILS AND ONE OF MY COLLEAGUES WILL CONTACT YOU...

One of the funniest 'most-embarrassing-moment' stories published by *New Woman* magazine in its competition pages was about a lady who picked up several items at a discount store. When she finally got to the checkout, she learned that one of her items had no price tag or barcode. Imagine her embarrassment when the checkout person got on the intercom and boomed out for the entire store to hear: "PRICE CHECK ON LANE THIRTEEN. TAMPAX, SUPER SIZE".

That was bad enough, but somebody at the rear of the store apparently misunderstood the word 'Tampax' for 'thumbtacks'. In a businesslike tone, a voice boomed back over the intercom: "DO YOU WANT THE KIND YOU PUSH IN WITH YOUR THUMBS OR THE KIND YOU POUND IN WITH A HAMMER?"

The chief at a hotel in Switzerland lost one of his fingers in a meat-cutting machine and, after a little shopping around, submitted a compensation claim to his insurance company. The company, suspecting negligence or even fraud, sent out one of its men to have a look for himself. He tried the machine and also lost a finger. The chef's claim was approved.

On Wednesday 29 March 2006, the Ryanair service from Liverpool to Londonderry landed at Ballykelly, a military airfield, by mistake. In a masterpiece of understatement, the pilot said: "We have arrived at the wrong airport". Ryanair sought to deflect criticism by saying that such a thing had never happened before.

One of the passengers complained, not because he now found himself in the wrong place, but because, he said: "They didn't let us go down the slide".

Be sure to cancel your credit cards before you die ...

A lady died in January 2006 and Citibank billed her for February and March with their annual service charges on her card account, adding late fees and interest on the monthly charge.

The balance had been $0 but was now somewhere around $60. A family member placed a call to Citibank.

Family member: I am calling to tell you she died in January.

Citibank: The account was never closed, so the late fees and charges still apply.

Fm: Maybe you should turn it over to collections.

C: Since it is two months overdue, it already has been.

Fm: So, what will they do when they find out she is dead?

C: Either report her account to Frauds Division or report her to the Credit Bureau – maybe both!

Fm: Do you think God will be mad at her?

C: Excuse me?

Fm: Did you just get what I was telling you – the part about her being dead?

C: Sir, you'll have to speak to my supervisor.

Supervisor: Can I help you?

Fm: I'm calling to tell you that she died in January.

S: The account was never closed, so the late fees and charges still apply. [We've heard this before somewhere – it must be a standard part of the Citibank script.]

Fm: Do you mean you want to collect from her estate?

S: Are you her lawyer?

Fm: No, I'm her great nephew.

S: Could you fax us a death certificate?

Fm: Sure. [Fax number is given.]

S: Our system just isn't set up for death. I don't know what more I can do to help.

Fm: Well, if you figure it out, great! If not, you could just keep billing her. I really don't think she will care.

S: Well, the late fees and charges do still apply. [What is wrong with these people?]

Fm: Would you like her new billing address?

S: Yes, that would help.

Fm: Odessa Memorial Cemetery, Highway 129, Plot number 69.

S: Sir, that's a cemetery!

Fm: What do you do with dead people on your planet?

AAAH.. THERE YOU ARE! I'M DEAD NOW, YOU SEE, AND I WANT YOU TO CANCEL MY CREDIT CARD.

During a shopping trip to a department store, I was looking around for a salesperson so I could pay for my purchase. Finally, I ran into a woman wearing the shop's ID tag and told her I was trying to locate a cashier.

"I can't help you," she briskly replied, barely slowing down. "I work in customer service."

From the 'All in a Day's Work' column Readers Digest

We are living in a world today where lemonade is made from artificial flavours and furniture polish is made from real lemons.

Alfred Newman

That junk mail just keeps on coming, even when you're dead:

- *Letter from Eastern Contracting: **"Dear Mrs Gronquist-Deceased. Refresh yourself with a shower from Eastern Contracting ... and, Mrs Gronquist-Deceased, you can take advantage of our six-month, interest-free credit"***

- *Cover of a holiday brochure sent to a vicar's widow: **"Tomorrow you could be in Paradise"** – she sent it back with the words **"He's already there"** scribbled on it*

- *A widow from Reading was sent a mock newspaper showing her husband, who died six months earlier, winning £1 million. He was quoted as saying: **"It's very hard to describe how I feel right now; in an instant my life has changed completely"***

- *A woman in Leeds received a sample of tampons addressed to her 90-year-old grandmother who had died the previous year.*

How to stop junk mail (whether you're alive or dead)

Some five million people in Britain have received direct mail addressed to a dead relative or close associate. Three million have taken action to prevent it happening again but the majority continue to be sent mail several times by the same companies, the worst offenders being catalogue companies, mail order clubs, utilities, holiday firms and financial services.

The Bereavement Register has been set up to enable people to register the details of their deceased relatives. Companies can check the register and remove from their mailing list anyone included on it. Not only is this beneficial for distressed relatives but it also stops businesses from sending out futile (and totally counter-productive) mailshots to dead people. The Bereavement Register can be contacted via the Internet on: www.the-bereavement-register.org.uk or on: 0870 600 7222.

Also, the Mailing Preference Service, set up by the Direct Marketing Association, legally obliges companies to remove the names and addresses of anyone who does not want to be on their mailing lists. You can register online at: www.mpsonline.org.uk or by calling: 0207 291 3310.

Dear Mr Hyde
Don't you ever stop moaning? Please take your custom elsewhere (you silly old sod). You need to get out more or see a doctor.

Handwritten response to a complaint letter received by the B&Q store in Farnborough, Hampshire. In fairness, a B&Q spokesman said: "We're absolutely shocked that this letter has been sent out. This is not the sort of thing we would ever write to our customers and we just don't know how it happened. Good customer service is very important to us and we are dismayed that this letter was sent to Mr Hyde. We have launched a senior level internal investigation to get to the bottom of this and to make sure it does not happen again".

A suicide hotline is where they talk to you until you don't feel like killing yourself. Exactly the opposite of telemarketing.

Dana Snow

They usually have two tellers in my local bank. Except when it's very busy, when they have one.

Rita Rudner

Let's learn from the Russians!

In Soviet times, when state-owned enterprises and shops had no obligation to compete, customers were often seen as a nuisance. Those attitudes still linger in smaller stores where assistants greet customers with "I'm listening!" or "Speak!"

In the 1990s Aeroflot, the state airline, tried to make light of its poor image with advertisements that boasted 'We don't smile because we are serious about making you happy'. The advert flopped but there is evidence of change.

Larger businesses are beginning to learn, despite their cultural belief, that the kind of duty smile favoured by Americans only signifies two things: white teeth and insincerity. But better a duty smile than duty rudeness and nowadays even the security guards at the GUM shopping centre are polite and helpful.

I was checking-out at the local Wal-Mart with just a few items and the lady behind me put her things on the belt close to mine. I picked up one of those dividers that they keep by the cash register and placed it between our things so they wouldn't get mixed.

After the checkout operator had scanned all of my items, she picked up the divider, looking it all over for the barcode so that she could scan it. Not finding a barcode she said to me: "Do you know how much this is?"

I said to her: "I've changed my mind, I don't think I'll buy that today".

She said: "OK", and I paid her for the things I'd purchased and left.

She had no clue to what had just happened.

Recently, when I went to McDonalds I saw on the menu that you could have an order of six, nine or 12 Chicken McNuggets. I asked for half a dozen McNuggets. "We don't have half a dozen nuggets," said the teenager at the counter. "You don't?" I replied. "We only have six, nine or 12," was the response.

"So I can't order half a dozen nuggets, but I can order six?"

"That's right."

So I shook my head and ordered six McNuggets.

'They're only puttin' in a nickel, but they want a dollar song'.

Song title that says it all about increasing customer expectations

The deadline for complaints was yesterday.

Notice in Deal hotel

Are prisoners 'customers'?

You would think they were if you read a report prepared by the Chief Inspector of Prisons in 2003 about conditions at Belmarsh Prison in south-east London which houses some of our most notorious criminals and terrorists.

Those who responded to a 'customer' survey at the 880-inmate prison made their displeasure clear as they accused staff of failing to show them adequate respect:

- 65% of respondents said the quality of the food was either bad or very bad

- 62% were dissatisfied with the choice of menus

- 66% considered the portions inadequate

- 73% complained they had to wait more than five minutes for somebody to arrive when they rang for attention

- Other inadequacies in the room service at Belmarsh included 40% of prisoners not receiving fresh sheets every week, while 45% criticised the lack of cleaning materials for their cells

- Other concerns included rude escort staff and uncomfortable vans being used to take prisoners to and from the jail. One prisoner took issue with the standard of driving, which was described as "appalling".

Widely reported at the time, Pete Cartwright, a member of the Prison Officers' Association's national executive, said his members were prevented from providing a good service by the poor staffing levels.

THE PARKING TICKET AWARDS

- In 2004 Nadhim Zahawi, founder of YouGov, was thrown from his motorbike in a nasty accident. As he was stretchered off with serious leg injuries into the ambulance, his crumpled scooter was given a £100 parking ticket by a traffic warden

- Retired blacksmith Robert McFarland of Skipton, North Yorkshire, found a parking ticket stuck to the nose of his horse, Charlie Boy. Under the heading 'Vehicle Description', the traffic warden had scribbled, 'brown horse'

- Pet shop owner Cliff Chamberlain from Eccles in Manchester was unloading his van and left a rabbit called Bugsy in its hutch outside the shop. Naturally, it was Bugsy who copped the fine

- Bus driver Chris O'Mahony was given a ticket for bringing the Number 77 Manchester to Moston service to a halt at a bus stop. The traffic warden simply joined the queue of embarking passengers, hopped on board and proudly handed over a sample of his best work.

For other stories about the delights of being a traffic warden, see The Parking Ticket Awards, compiled by Barrie Segal (£6:99, but double if you don't pay within a fortnight).

Lost in translation!

It's not unknown for medical secretaries to get it wrong – with consequences that could be just hilarious, but could be much worse. Some of these 'mistranslations' occur because the secretary is unfamiliar with English, but they can also happen because of poor telephone skills or even because the 'spellcheck' programme has been allowed to operate without hindrance.

- *Information about a patient's 'phlebitis in his left leg' was typed out as 'flea bite his left leg'*

- *A 'below knee amputation' was transcribed as 'baloney amputation'*

- *'Eustachian tube [in the ear] malfunction' was given as 'Euston station tube malfunction'*

- *'Examination of genitalia reveals that he is circus sized'*

- *'Whilst in Casualty, she was examined, X-rated and sent home'.*

HANG ON REARVIEW MIRROR

VISITOR

This pass does not guarantee a parking space
In the interest of road safety on the campus
you will be ticketed if you:

✳ Park outside a marked bay ✳

✳ Park in a disabled bay without
displaying a valid disabled badge ✳

✳ Fail to display this permit as specified ✳

✳ Penalty £80 (£40 if paid within 14 days) ✳

Please write the name of the conference, meeting
or other event you are attending, or the name
and department of the person you are visiting:

Please hang this permit from your interior
driving mirror with this side facing the windscreen.

DATE	No.
- 2 MAR 2007	1075

UNIVERSITY OF
Chichester

Any alterations to the details will invalidate this permit.

A warm welcome from one of our newer universities - you'd think they would need all the friends they can get

What can happen when you don't focus on the customer ...

Leroy Greer is a bit of a romantic. He sent a dozen roses and a teddy bear to his girlfriend, with a card reading "Just wanted to say I love you".

Unfortunately the florist sent the receipt to his wife.

Now the luxury car salesman from Missouri City is suing the firm for $1 million for "mental anguish" caused by the mix-up and his resultant divorce.

The affair was laid bare after his wife received a receipt from the website greetings business. Bereft of bouquet, she called the company and requested more information, which not only included the damning card message but the girlfriend's name and address.

She faxed the receipt to her husband at work, plus an appropriate message, and divorce proceedings followed swiftly.

Mr Greer has blamed the florist for his divorce and insisted it had told him no receipt would be sent to his home.

The company says that it takes "all matters relating to our customers seriously", but adds that "we are not responsible for an individual's personal conduct".

Newspaper report, August 2007. Interesting to speculate on the words Mrs Greer used when faxing the florist's receipt to her husband.

Stories about customers and customer service experiences

Darwin-defying customers - the evidence that disproves natural selection

By Ted Johns

As observers of the customer service scene, we spend too much time thinking about the doziness of some (only a few!) of the people employed in customer service roles and revelling in stories like these:

- *Customer in shoe shop, holding up pair of shoes: "Have you got these in a bigger size?" Assistant: "What, both of them?"*

- *Customer, fingering tablecloth: "Is it reversible?" Assistant: "No, but you can use both sides."*

What we don't do is tell stories about our own stupidity and confess to our own inadequacies – the type of ineptitude that makes customer-facing staff talk about us behind our backs whenever they are gathered together for purposes of group therapy.

Yet the fact remains that we customers aren't very bright and some of us are downright dim. If you doubt it (and I suspect you probably do so far as you're concerned, even if you are prepared simultaneously to believe that the rest of the human race is largely composed of congenital dimwits), take heart from the words of Sir Callum McCarthy, chairman of the Financial Services Authority, who has 'research' to 'prove' that a goodly number of UK citizens are just too thick to make financial decisions. This is what he has to say:

"Among the adult population, if presented with the *Yellow Pages* and asked to name a plumber, 23% cannot do so. More than 20%, if asked to choose between receiving £30 or 10% of £350 choose the lower figure. Put another way, more than one in five of adults would not have understood either of the last two sentences."

Let's bear in mind here that Sir Callum has an axe to grind. It is clearly in his interests to show that the unwashed British public is incapable of acting thoughtfully and rationally. Armed with this 'evidence', he can justify the existence – nay, the expansion – of the Financial Services Authority, whose purpose is to protect us from mis-selling and other horrors while also making sure that companies come clean about interest rates and the fine print of their mortgage offers.

He does have a point, though. No wonder that some people have such problems with deciphering car insurance paperwork, the assembly instructions for an Ikea wardrobe, the rules for planning applications and even the forms produced by the Financial Services Authority. Clearly it's not because these forms, offers, instructions and rules are unnecessarily complicated, verbose and legalistic – it's because we're thick. So it's our fault and, what's more, nothing can be done about it because when you're thick, you're thick for life. It's not just a matter of being ignorant (which is quite different from being thick), which could be put right with some reader-friendly, approachable, accessible and readily-available knowledge. No: it's because you're stupid, stupid.

If customers are thick or stupid or ignorant, then obviously they have to be protected from those who are cleverer than they are, who might otherwise use their cleverness in ways that are wicked. Hence the justification for regulatory agencies that are intended to prevent us from being baffled by 'science', overwhelmed by explanatory literature that does not explain and submerged by 'promises' which turn out to be written on sand just as the tide is coming in.

Thus there are two things that keep the regulators in business. The first, as we have seen, is that customers are often thick or ignorant. The second is that some organisations aren't as honest and straightforward as they might be, but seem to devote a good deal of their energies to outwitting their regulators. One of the ways they can do this is through a technique known as 'confusion marketing', where prices and 'deals' are presented to us in such a mixture that it becomes virtually impossible to make sensible choices. Equally widespread is what I call 'confusion semantics', in which a phrase that looks as though it might mean something worthwhile actually doesn't mean that at all. Many otherwise competent citizens – who can walk, talk and chew gum all at the same time – have fallen for claims about '24-hour service', believing it to mean that somebody is available to give them assistance at any hour of the day or night, when what it means in practice is that someone will answer the phone within 24 hours.

If we're all thick, and over 20% of us are, surely we're confused enough as it is, without any 'confusion marketing' or 'confusion semantics' to add to our distress.

Dear Sir

Sorry payment is late. I have just been informed my mother has just died and good riddance. Payment will be along shortly. Please give me a break, it has just slipped my mind, sorry. I'm sorry for what I have said about my mother, you don't know her like I do. Thank you.

Email received by water utility company from one of its customers

The second most asked question of cast members is: "What time is the 3 o'clock parade?"

Jim Cunningham, Disney Corporation

When customers are buying products, they are largely unconscious.

Part of a student's answer in a business studies examination

On what days is your Sunday brunch available?

Customer phone call to a well-known restaurant

Caller to RAC Motoring Services:
Does your European Breakdown Policy cover me when I'm travelling in Australia?

Operator:
Doesn't the product name give you a clue?

A store manager overheard a clerk saying to a customer: "No, ma'am, we haven't had any for some weeks now and it doesn't look as if we'll be getting any soon".

Alarmed by what was being said, the manager rushed over to the customer, who was walking out the door, and said: "That isn't true, madam. Of course we'll have some soon. In fact, we placed an order for it a couple of weeks ago".

Then the manager drew the clerk aside and growled: "Never, never say we don't have something. If we don't have it, say we ordered it and it's on its way. Now, what was it she wanted?"

"Rain."

Pack your computer away, you're not fit to own one ...

A woman calls the Canon help desk about problems with her printer. The tech asks her if she is "running it under Windows".

"No," replies the customer, " my desk is next to the door. But that's a good point. The man in the cubicle next to me is under a window and his is working fine".

Caller to Samsung Electronics: Can you give me the telephone number for Jack?

Operator: I'm sorry, sir, I don't understand who you're talking about.

Caller: On page 1, section 5, of the User Guide, it clearly states that I need to unplug the fax machine from the AC wall socket and telephone jack before cleaning. Now, can you give me the number for Jack?

Operator: I think it means the telephone point on the wall.

The help desk gave me a call from Major So-and-so who was having a problem with his work station. I spoke with him and he told me: "Every time I switch it over to 'official', the damn screen goes blank". I went down to see what the Hell this 'official' switch was. After nearly getting court-martialled for laughing so hard, I spent about 20 minutes explaining to this ex-pilot that 'off' was not an abbreviation for 'official'.

Tech Support: How much free space do you have on your hard drive?

Customer: Well, my wife likes to get on that Internet, and she downloaded 10 hours of free space. Is that enough?

Tech Support: I need you to right-click on the Open Desktop.

Customer: OK.

Tech Support: Did you get a pop-up menu?

Customer: No.

Tech Support: OK. Right click again. Do you see a pop-up menu?

Customer: No.

Tech Support: OK, sir. Can you tell me what you have done up until this point?

Customer: Sure. You told me to write 'Click', and so I wrote 'Click'.

Tech Support: OK. In the bottom left hand side of the screen, can you see the 'OK' button displayed?

Customer: Wow. How can you see my screen from there?

Caller: *The coffee cup holder on my computer is broken. Can I get a replacement, please?*

Help Desk: *I'm not sure what you mean. Where exactly is this coffee cup holder?*

Caller: *Well, there's a button on the front of my computer and when I press it a drink caddy pops out. You know, it's just like the ones they put in cars.*

Help Desk: *Sir, I think you'll find that's the CD slot.*

Customer: I deleted a file from my PC last week and I have just realised that I need it. If I turn my system clock back two weeks will I have my file back again?

When all else fails ...

An Australian boomerang company is understandably cynical about the ability or willingness of customers to read instructions. On each packet containing a boomerang is written this advice: 'This boomerang is guaranteed to return to you if thrown strictly in accordance with the enclosed instructions'.

The same message is repeated on the wrapper around the boomerang.

On the boomerang itself is a final sticker:
'NOW, READ THE BLOODY INSTRUCTIONS'.

Caller to Directory Enquiries: *I'd like the number of the Argoed Fish Bar in Cardiff, please.*

Operator: *I'm sorry, there's no such listing. Is the spelling correct?*

Caller: *Well, it used to be called the Bargoed Fish Bar, but the 'B' fell off.*

Caller: *I'd like to borrow £2,000.*

Bank operator: *Certainly, sir. Over how long?*

Caller: *Three years, please.*

Bank operator: *That will be £75 per month for 36 months. Is that OK?*

Caller: *No, not at all. I want it all at once.*

Customer: *I've been ringing 0700 2300 for two days and can't get through to enquiries. Can you help?*

Operator: *Where did you get that number from, sir?*

Customer: *It was on the door to the Travel Centre.*

Operator: *Sir, they are the opening hours.*

Then there was the caller who asked for a knitwear company in Woven.

Operator: Woven? Are you sure?

Caller: Yes, that's what it says on the label: Woven in Scotland.

Wacky warnings: given that some people are really stupid, it's not surprising that product instructions try to anticipate the very worst that the customer can do:

DO NOT put any person in this washer
Instruction accompanying a new washing machine

Never use a lit match or open flame to check fuel level
Advice from a car engine manufacturer

Please do not use this directory while operating a moving vehicle
Rules for the use of a phone book

WARNING: Remove child before folding
Instructions on a pushchair

I work in the home delivery enquiries (read: complaints) department of a major UK catalogue retailer. A colleague once took a call from an extremely disappointed woman who had purchased a cat gym/scratching type of thing. In the catalogue, the product is pictured with two little kittens climbing on it. You can probably guess what her complaint was ... yes, the product had been delivered, but the two cats weren't inside the box. The adviser explained politely that the picture was for illustration purposes only and that there was no way that we could send live animals via a parcel delivery service. However the customer continued to rant at him, threatening to report the complaint to Trading Standards, the press, her solicitors, etc. If that item is featured again, maybe we should add the phrase 'livestock not included' to the description.

More from the front line of computer wizardry ...

I had been doing tech support for Hewlett-Packard's DeskJet division for about a month when I had a customer call with a problem I just couldn't solve. She could not print yellow. All the other colours would print fine, which truly baffled me because the only true colours are cyan, magenta and yellow. For instance, green is a combination of cyan and yellow, but green printed fine. Every colour of the rainbow printed fine except for yellow.

I had the customer change ink cartridges. I had the customer delete and reinstall the drivers. Nothing worked. I asked my co-workers for help; they offered no new ideas. After two hours of trouble-shooting, I was about to tell the customer to send the printer back to us for repair when she asked quietly: "Should I try printing on a piece of white paper instead of this yellow paper?"

9-1-1 is 9-9-9 translated into American

Dispatcher: 9-1-1. What is your emergency?

Caller: I heard what sounded like gunshots coming from the brown house on the corner.

Dispatcher: Do you have an address?

Caller: No, I have on a blouse and slacks. Why?

Dispatcher: 9-1-1. What is your emergency?

Caller: I'm trying to reach 9-11 but my phone doesn't have an 11 on it.

Dispatcher: This is 9-11.

Caller: I thought you said it was 9-1-1.

Dispatcher: Yes, ma'am, 9-1-1 and 9-11 are the same thing.

Caller: Honey, I may be old, but I'm not stupid.

Dispatcher: 9-1-1.

Caller: Yeah, I'm having trouble breathing. I'm all out of breath. Darn – I think I'm going to pass out.

Dispatcher: Sir, where are you calling from?

Caller: I'm at a pay phone. North and Foster.

Dispatcher: Sir, an ambulance is on the way. Are you an asthmatic?

Caller: No.

Dispatcher: What were you doing before you started having trouble breathing?

Caller: Running from the police.

Police reveal that a woman arrested for shoplifting had a whole salami in her underwear. When asked why, she said it was because she was missing her Italian boyfriend.

Manchester Evening News

Now it's serious, because people like these have the vote

Q: Name a song with 'moon' in the title
A: Blue Suede Moon

Q: Name a bird with a long neck
A: Naomi Campbell

Q: Name something that floats in the bath
A: Water

Q: Name a famous royal
A: Mail

Q: Name something that flies but doesn't have an engine
A: A bicycle with wings

Q: Name something a cat does
A: Goes to the toilet

Q: Name something you do in the bathroom
A: Decorate

Q: Name a famous Scotsman
A: Jock

Q: Name a part of the body beginning with 'N'
A: Knee

Q: Name something you open other than a door
A: Your bowels

Answers given by contestants on Family Fortunes

Adventures with the WordPerfect Helpline

Help Desk: Ridge Hall computer assistance; may I help you?

Caller: Yes, well, I'm having trouble with WordPerfect.

HD: What sort of trouble?

C: Well, I was just typing along and all of a sudden the words went away.

HD: Went away?

C: They disappeared.

HD: Hmmmm. So what does your screen look like now?

C: Nothing.

HD: Nothing?

C: It's a blank; it won't accept anything when I type.

HD: Are you still in WordPerfect or did you get out?

C: How do I tell?

HD: Can you see the 'C': prompt on the screen?

C: What's a sea-prompt?

HD: Never mind. Can you move your cursor around the screen?

C: There isn't any cursor. I told you, it won't accept anything I type.

HD: Does your monitor have a power indicator?

C: What's a monitor?

HD: It's the thing with the screen on it that looks like a TV. Does it have a little light that tells you when it's on?

C: The light's not on.

HD: Can you find the power cable that comes out of the back of your monitor?

C: OK, here it is.

HD: Follow it for me and tell me if it's plugged securely into the back of your computer.

C: I can't reach.

HD: Uh huh. Well, can you see if it is?

C: No.

HD: Even if you maybe put your knee on something and leant way over?

C: Oh, it's not because I don't have the right angle – it's because it's dark.

HD: Dark?

C: Yes – the office light is off and the only light I have is coming in from the window.

HD: Well, turn on the office light, then.

C: I can't.

HD: No? Why not?

C: Because there's a power failure.

HD: A power – a power failure? Aha, okay, we've got it licked now. Do you still have the boxes and manuals and packing stuff your computer came in?

C: Well, yes, I keep them in the wardrobe.

HD: Good. Go get them, unplug your system and pack it up just like it was when you got it. Then take it back to the store you bought it from.

C: Really? Is it that bad?

HD: Yes, I'm afraid it is.

C: Well, all right then, I suppose. What do I tell them?

HD: Tell them you're too f***ing stupid to own a computer.

I can't get my wheelie bin up my back passage as it is too long and narrow.

Customer complaint about the refuse collection service in Lincolnshire

A man attempting to set up his new printer called the printer's tech support number, complaining about the error message: 'Can't find the printer!' On the phone, the man said he had even held the printer up in front of the screen, but the computer still couldn't find it.

Brain: an apparatus with which we think we think. *Ambrose Bierce*

Delivery dilemma

Help Desk: Hello, Help Desk here, how can I help you?

Caller: Yes, this is Mr Gerber in Administration. I've received a memo about this new requirement to shut down our computers at night.

Help Desk: That's correct. Do you know how to properly shut down your computer?

Caller: Of course I do. I'm not an idiot. But I don't think this is a very good idea. I'll miss a lot of important emails.

Help Desk: I'm not sure I understand the problem.

Caller: I get a lot of email that's sent overnight and I'll miss all of that if the computer isn't left on.

My neighbour works in the operations department in the central office of a large bank. Employees in the field call him when they have problems with their computers. One night he got a call from a woman in one of the branch banks who had this question: "I've got smoke coming from the back of my terminal. Do you guys have a fire downtown?"

Police in Radnor, Pennsylvania, interrogated a suspect by placing a metal colander on his head and connecting it with wires to a photocopier. The message 'He's lying' was placed in the copier and police pressed the copy button each time they thought the suspect wasn't telling the truth. Believing the 'lie detector' was genuine, the suspect confessed.

More stories from the world of Help Desks ...

One Help Desk received a fax with a note on the bottom asking for it to be faxed back to the sender when they were finished with it because he needed to file it.

Customer: Can you copy the Internet for me on this diskette?

Tech Support: All right. Try double-clicking on the 'File Manager' icon.

Customer: That's why I hate Windows – the icons. I'm a Protestant and don't believe in icons.

Tech Support: Well, that's an industry term, sir. I don't believe it was meant to ...

Customer: I don't care about any industry terms. I don't believe in icons.

Tech Support: (cunningly) Well ... why don't you click on to the little picture of a filing cabinet. Is 'little picture' OK?

Customer: (click) Terrific!

When you go into court you are putting your fate into the hands of twelve people who weren't smart enough to get out of jury duty.

Norm Crosby

WE HAVE A CRIMINAL JURY SYSTEM WHICH IS SUPERIOR TO ANY IN THE WORLD AND ITS EFFICIENCY IS ONLY MARRED BY THE DIFFICULTY OF FINDING TWELVE PEOPLE EVERY DAY WHO DON'T KNOW ANYTHING AND CAN'T READ.

Mark Twain

Stories from the water industry ...

Several months ago a customer called regarding high consumption on her water bill. She wondered if there was a misread on her meter. The agent advised her that her meter was in the airing cupboard, according to the company's records.

The customer insisted on finding it while still on the phone, even though she wasn't sure what the meter looked like. The sound of rummaging was deafening as she clambered around in the cupboard under the stairs.

"Is this it?" she eventually said.

The agent advised her that she should be looking for a box against the wall with dials on the front.

"I can't see any dials on it, dear, but it does have some letters."

"That may be the manufacturer of the meter – what does it say?"

"Dyson."

These people may be on quiz shows, but they're customers too and let's not forget it.

FORT BOYARD

Jodie Marsh: Arrange these two groups of letters to form a word – CHED and PIT.
Team: Chedpit.

LINCS FM PHONE-IN

Presenter: Which is the largest Spanish-speaking country in the world?
Contestant: Barcelona.
Presenter: I was really after the name of a country.
Contestant: I'm sorry, I don't know the names of any countries in Spain.

JAMES O'BRIEN SHOW (LBC)

O'Brien: How many kings of England have been called Henry?
Contestant: Er, well, I know there was a Henry the Eighth ... er ... er ... three?

KELLY TODAY (ITV)

Lorraine Kelly: How many days in a leap year?
Contestant: 253.

LUNCHTIME SHOW (BMRB)

Presenter: What religion was Guy Fawkes?
Contestant: Jewish.
Presenter: That's close enough.

PHIL WOOD SHOW (BBC GMR)

Wood: What 'K' would describe the Islamic Bible?
Contestant: Er ...
Wood: It's got two syllables ... Kor ...
Contestant: Blimey?
Wood: Ha ha ha ha, no. The past participle of run ...
Contestant: (silence)
Wood: OK, try it another way. Today I run, yesterday I ...
Contestant: Walked?

GWR FM (Bristol)

Presenter: What happened in Dallas on November 22, 1963?
Contestant: I don't know. I wasn't watching it then.

DARYL DENHAM'S DRIVETIME (VIRGIN RADIO)

Daryl Denham: In which country would you spend shekels?
Contestant: Holland?
Denham: Try the next letter of the alphabet.
Contestant: Iceland? Ireland?
Denham (helpfully): It's a bad line. Did you say Israel?
Contestant: No.

UNIVERSITY CHALLENGE

Bamber Gascoigne: What was Gandhi's first name?
Contestant: Goosey, goosey?

THE WEAKEST LINK

Anne Robinson: In traffic, what 'J' is where two roads meet?
Contestant: Jool carriageway?

DANNY KELLY SHOW (RADIO WM)

Kelly: Which French Mediterranean town hosts a famous film festival every year?
Contestant: I don't know, I need a clue.
Kelly: OK. What do beans come in?
Contestant: Cartons?

BEG, BORROW OR STEAL (BBC 2)

Jamie Theakston: Where do you think Cambridge University is?
Contestant: Geography isn't my strong point.
Theakston: There's a clue in the title.
Contestant: Leicester.

MAGIC 52 (NE England)

Presenter: In what year was President Kennedy assassinated?
Contestant: Erm ...
Presenter: Well, let's put it this way – he didn't see 1964.
Contestant: 1965?

Stories about customers and customer service experiences

It's somehow reassuring to know that stories about poor service are not particularly new. This letter, from Mary Shield of Hyde Park Gardens, London W2, appeared in *The Times* on 19 August 1947.

I have just been dictating the following telegram over the telephone: "Caledonian Hotel, Edinburgh. Coming tomorrow one night only due 9.59 pm. Mary Shield".

At the word "due" the operator (a young man) said: "One moment, please".

A considerable pause and a girl operator took over. The young man had gone off duty!

No wonder we're in the mess we are.

Leaving aside the fact that nobody nowadays knows what a telegram is, we can all recognise the concept of an employee who is such a keen clock-watcher that he stops what he's doing at the precise moment his shift ends, even if he's in the middle of a conversation with his customer. OK, we're better off than we were in 1947 – we could hardly be worse off – but some things never change. Comforting, isn't it?

Anne Robinson: Which activity, which can be primary, secondary, higher, further or adult, is mainly conducted in schools or universities?

Contestant: Pass.

The Weakest Link

> I was in a car dealership a while ago, when a large motor home was towed into the garage. The front of the vehicle was in dire need of repair and the whole thing generally looked like an extra in 'Twister'.
>
> I asked the manager what had happened. He told me that the driver had set the 'cruise control' and then went in the back to make a sandwich.

Oz sun frazzles brains - unless they were frazzled to start with

We keep being told that even Australian footballers are human beings, but it's advice that's hard to swallow in view of the way they conduct themselves, if the following remarks are anything to go by ...

"I owe a lot to my parents, especially my mother and father."

(Shane Wakelin)

"Nobody in football should be called a genius. A genius is a guy like Norman Einstein."

(Mick Malthouse-Collingwood)

"You guys line up alphabetically by height and you guys pair up in groups of three, then line up in a circle."

(Barry Hall, Captain of the Sydney team, trying to organise his team for some training sessions)

"I can't really remember the names of the clubs we went to."

(Brock Maclean of Melbourne, on being asked whether he had visited the pyramids during his stay in Egypt)

"I've never had major knee surgery on any other part of my body."

(Luke Darcy)

"I never comment on referees and I'm not going to break the habit of a lifetime for that prat."

(Terry Wallace)

"Strangely, in slow motion replay, the ball seemed to hang in the air for even longer."

(Dermott Brereton)

"That kick was absolutely unique, except for the one before it which was identical."

(Dermott Brereton – again)

"I would not say he [Chris Judd] is the best centreman in the Australian Football League, but there are none better."

(Dermott Brereton yet again – clearly he needs watching)

Companies can be stupid, too

I n 2006, the National Consumer Council published its by now celebrated report, *The Stupid Company: How British Businesses Throw Away Money by Alienating Consumers*. The research highlighted five ways that companies get it wrong:

1. **Inflated expectations and broken promises**

   The stupid company over-promises and under-delivers. It may focus on today's sale at the expense of longer-term damage to its reputation; its advertising creates false (and sometimes unattainable) expectations; and its business practices permit sales people to make wild promises

2. **Sell, sell, sell**

   The stupid company is obsessive about making a sale, even though its efforts are often counter-productive, especially when existing customers are neglected in favour of special deals for new customers

3. **Sneaky and dishonest**

   The stupid company believes it can succeed by misleading customers and then being underhand and evasive. Unsurprisingly, customers do not welcome such behaviour, even though it gives them an excuse to retaliate by adopting similar strategies themselves, e.g. when falsifying or exaggerating insurance claims or complaining needlessly about package holidays

4. **Impersonal and robotic**

   The stupid company appears distant from consumers and deals with them in a clinical and sometimes uncaring manner. Customers react badly when it seems to them that the organisation is trying to fob them off with excuses, or shift the problem elsewhere, or produce so-called responses or explanations that miss the point of the customer's grievance altogether

5. **Incompetent and ineffectual**

   The stupid company is slow moving, patronising and apparently incapable of getting the easy things right. Sometimes organisations do manage to pull the wool over consumers' eyes by behaving in a highly manipulative and misleading manner but, startlingly, the NCC says that: "All too often their actions have the smell of incompetence about them," and "it is hard to avoid the conclusion that, even if they were trying hard to mislead consumers, a sizeable number of companies wouldn't be any good at it". In fact, I believe this is less to do with the stupidity of businesses and more to do with the increasing sophistication of consumers plus the growing presence of watchdog and other regulatory agencies.

By contrast, the smart business will do five things:

1. **Provide continuity and ownership**

   In a smart business, the same member of staff deals with an individual customer from start to finish, provides personal details so that further contact can be maintained and tries to resolve any difficulties on a 'one-stop-shop' basis, i.e. without passing the customer on needlessly to someone else

2. **Show respect and honesty**

   The smart business is straight about things like product availability, the need (or otherwise) for extended warranties, delivery times and the advantages and disadvantages of alternative routes for resolving whatever the customer's need or problem happens to be

3. **Give the personal touch**

   The smart business encourages its staff to treat customers like individuals and to show initiative. In a smart hotel, the receptionist can exercise his or her discretion when handling guest complaints. At Timpsons, the key-cutting and shoe-repairing chain, shop staff have the authority to dispense compensation of up to £500 without reference to anyone at head office

4. **Reward existing customers**

   We already know that it costs much more to attract new customers than to keep existing ones – and your existing customers are always a potential marketing opportunity given that they can become your 'active promoters', encouraging their friends, relatives and colleagues to become your customers as well. So why do so few organisations provide incentives for customer loyalty and why are so many seemingly indifferent when their existing customers defect?

5. **Provide aftercare**

   The smart business does not forget its customers after they've bought something; instead, it checks that they are still happy. It's customary in restaurants for the staff to ask if you're happy with the food, but it's not so common for, say, a solicitor to ask clients if they are happy with the service provided.

Read the stories in this chapter and be prepared to reflect on what the National Consumer Council has to say.

My Promise To You:

Best Price
Best Selection
Friendliest Service
Fast, Free Delivery
And a little bit o' me on every mattress I sell!

Poster in window of bedding shop, USA

My friend is always impressed by the customer service in McDonalds, but has to admit that sometimes their reliance on scripts lets them down. He went into the Liverpool Street branch and received the customary McDonalds' greeting: "Yeah?"

"A pack of fries, please," says my friend.

"Would you like a pack of fries with that?", replies the McDonalds robot, reading from his lines on the back of the cash register.

The only employees who are really customer-orientated are the detectives in a department store.

Rheinhard Sprenger, speaking at the European Association of Personnel Managers, June 1995

Too many staff have got their noses pressed up against the career ladder and their backsides facing the customer.

Jack Welch, one-time Chief Executive Officer, General Electric

YOU DON'T HAVE TO BE MAD TO WORK HERE.

In 1999, confronting serious problems, Marks & Spencer launched a 'Smile of the Week' award, with a budget of £1 million with which to give recognition to staff around the company's stores. It was reported that the judges were struggling to find suitable recipients – only one girl qualified at the beginning and it turned out that she only smiled because she had wind.

Used Cars
Why go elsewhere to be cheated?
Come here first.

Small ad, motoring magazine, USA

PLEASE REMEMBER THAT WE ARE WORKING 24 HOURS A DAY, SEVEN DAYS A YEAR, ON BEHALF OF OUR CUSTOMERS.

Letter from Powergen

The perils of translation ...

Scandinavian vacuum manufacturer Electrolux used the following in an American ad campaign: 'Nothing sucks like an Electrolux'.

NOTHING SUCKS LIKE ELECTROLUX!

In Taiwan, the translation of the Pepsi slogan, 'Come alive with the Pepsi generation', came out as 'Pepsi will bring your ancestors back from the dead'.

Chicken-man Frank Perdue's slogan, 'It takes a tough man to make tender chicken', got terribly mangled in translation to Spanish. A picture of Mr Perdue with one of his chickens appeared on billboards all over Mexico with the caption: 'It takes a hard man to make a chicken affectionate'.

Extract from a Tokyo car rental brochure: 'When a passenger of foot heace in sight, tootle the horn. Trumpet him melodiously at first, but if he still obstracles your passage then tootle him with vigour'.

An American T-shirt manufacturer in Miami printed shirts in Spanish for the Spanish market during the Pope's visit. However, instead of the desired 'I saw the Pope', it read 'I saw the Potato'.

Ford launched their Pinto model in Brazil only to find that 'Pinto' is slang for 'tiny male genitals'.

When Parker Pen marketed a ballpoint pen in Mexico, its ads were designed to say: 'It won't leak in your pocket and embarrass you'. However, the company used the Spanish word 'embarazar' for 'embarrass' - so the ad read: 'It won't leak in your pocket and make you pregnant'.

We know that communication is a problem, but the company is not going to discuss it with the employees.

Switching supervisor, AT & T, Long Lines Division

Contact us if you have had any of these:

- **Heart Attack**

- **Fatal Heart Attack**

- **Stroke**

- **Arythmia.**

Advertisement for Quantum Claims

I'm not conceited.
Conceit is a fault and I have no faults.

David Lee Roth. Some companies are like this, suffering from 'pronoia'.
If 'paranoia' is the mistaken belief you have enemies, 'pronoia' is the
mistaken belief you have friends.

See places that no longer exist.

Proud boast in the brochure for a coach
tour company, Charleston, South Carolina

A letter from the consumer council Postwatch in response to a recent complaint contained the 'hope that this levitates your concerns'.

I feel my burden has been lifted already.

Letter in The Times

Illiterate?
Write today for free help.

Small ad, Chichester Observer

Irish police are being handicapped in their search for a stolen van because they cannot issue a description. It's a Special Branch vehicle and they don't want the public to know what it looks like.

The Guardian

A US soldier in the closing years of World War Two, with a dreary desk job filling in forms, tried to make his life more interesting by listing all the sticky fly-papers in his mess hall and giving a code reference number to each.

He then started to keep a weekly record of the fly mortality rate, sending figures back to the Pentagon recording the number of flies on each flypaper, the point at which the flypapers were renewed, the location of each flypaper and so forth.

After a while this too became boring, so he stopped. He then began to receive sharp notes from Washington demanding why he hadn't filed his flypaper returns.

For some years, the inhabitants of the Berkshire village of East Ilsley had been complaining to the Post Office that it was impossible to post large envelopes through the tiny slot of their village postbox. Finally their MP received this reply from the Acting Head Postmaster at Reading:

"A recent check, made when the box was emptied on a Monday morning, revealed that 40 items had been posted and none of the items were observed to be large enough to have caused difficulty when posting. The evidence I have indicates, therefore, that there has been no complaint about the posting aperture being too small and that the box is more than adequate for the number of letters found to be posted."

And, of course, the postman had absolutely no trouble with the big letters that weren't in there.

Warning: Read the Warning Labels

On a helmet-mounted mirror used by US cyclists:
REMEMBER – OBJECTS IN THE MIRROR ARE ACTUALLY BEHIND YOU

On a packet of Sainsbury's salted peanuts:
WARNING – CONTAINS NUTS

On a Marks & Spencer's bread and butter pudding:
WARNING – PRODUCT WILL BE HOT AFTER HEATING

Instructions with a Rowenta electric iron:
WARNING – NEVER IRON CLOTHES ON THE BODY

On an insect spray purchased in New Zealand:
THIS PRODUCT NOT TESTED ON ANIMALS

On a hairdryer purchased from Sears, Roebuck:
DO NOT USE WHILE SLEEPING

On a bag of Fritos:
YOU COULD BE A WINNER! NO PURCHASE NECESSARY. DETAILS INSIDE

On a Swedish chainsaw:
DO NOT ATTEMPT TO STOP CHAIN WITH YOUR HANDS

On a child's Superman costume:
WEARING THIS GARMENT DOES NOT ENABLE YOU TO FLY

On a Korean kitchen knife:
KEEP OUT OF CHILDREN

On a Japanese product used to relieve painful haemorrhoids:
LIE DOWN ON BED AND INSERT POSCOOL SLOWLY UP TO THE PROJECTED PORTION LIKE A SWORD-GUARD INTO ANAL DUCT. WHILE INSERTING POSCOOL FOR APPROXIMATELY FIVE MINUTES, KEEP QUIET.

By Ted Johns

So, if you want to know more about neutering and why it's best for you and your dog, give us a call.

Advert for the National Canine Defence League

Service overkill

My wife was on a business trip and I was expecting her to arrive home tonight. Then I received this phone call:

Caller: Hello, this is British Airways. Is Ms Showalter there?

Respondent: Um, no, she's not home yet. Is there a problem?

Caller: OK, well, can I leave a message for her?

Respondent: Sure. Is there something wrong? As far as I know, she's on one of your flights right now.

Caller: We just wanted to let her know that her flight is going to be arriving a little late. It will be arriving in Philadelphia at 7.45.

Respondent: The one she's on?

Caller: Yes.

Respondent: You want me to tell her when she gets home that her flight arrived late?

Caller: Yes.

Respondent: OK, I'll let her know.

Caller: Thank you, sir.

Restoring the balance - stories that fill your heart with wonder

By Ted Johns

Writing in the *Sunday Telegraph*, Miriam Gross tells us that a cruel new word has entered the language to describe women who no longer have any sex appeal. The word is 'invisible' used as a noun, as in 'I left the party early; there were so many invisibles'.

Many people delivering customer service in 'front line' roles are already treated as if they were invisible, whether they are male or female, equipped or otherwise with sex appeal. And by the way, 'front line' is a completely inappropriate yet strangely resonant phrase when applied to customer service. It arouses connotations of World War One, with service staff in the trenches, the enemy (customers) in those trenches over there and a kind of zero-contact No Man's Land in between. Any minute now, the whistle will blow, the customers will come at us and it's up to us to get them first. No wonder so much customer service is confrontational.

As Miriam says, being 'invisible' applies to all sorts of customer service roles, 'and thousands like them in other jobs, [who] should of course be looked up to rather than straight through'.

She's right. She also says that in a supermarket she seeks out the checkout whose operator is a woman, preferably grey-haired and without much make-up, because such people are typically faster and more efficient than younger females or men of any age. Whether she's right about that is a matter of taste but supermarket checkouts do demonstrate how customer service can make the difference between keeping customers or driving them away. For this reason alone it is never sensible for businesses to neglect, undermine or denigrate the customer service function or the people who work in it, since it is they who have the power (if they choose to exercise it) to turn casual customers into loyal advocates. Or not.

When I led some consultancy assignments for a major supermarket in the 1990s, we sought to establish what checkout operators were for. We already knew what they *do*, but that wasn't the important issue. They could be very efficient at passing goods through the scanner, checking money-off vouchers, opening those tricky plastic bags and folding the receipt round the customer's credit card but still be hopeless checkout operators when judged against the aims of the business. How could this be?

It's because the right question to ask about any employee is not "What do you *do*?" but rather "What are you *for*?" Strictly speaking, nobody (including you and me) is paid to *do* anything at all. They (again including you and me) are paid to **achieve** things, to make a contribution, to make a difference; in the final analysis to **add value**.

The question "What do you do?" is irrelevant and the answer is equally irrelevant when judging the employee's performance. Things go wrong, however, because too many organisations are hypnotised by a job description mentality. Job descriptions typically list the *tasks* the employee is meant to perform and often ignore the purpose of the job altogether or state the purpose in such a depressing and bureaucratic way that nobody can get excited about it.

If you suffer from insomnia I recommend that you keep a copy of your job description beside your bed. Start reading it at 2 o'clock in the morning and I guarantee that within five minutes you will be in a coma.

So if "What are you *for*?" is the only important question so far as checkout operators in a supermarket are concerned, what is the answer? Well, the real purpose – the only added-value function – for the checkout operator is **to make the customer want to come back**. That is what they are for. Of course, they perform some essential tasks along the way and they must make sure these tasks are undertaken efficiently, smoothly and quickly (customers usually expect these things), but above all they must create the kind of physical/emotional 'experience' for the customer which makes the customer think that this supermarket is a pleasant place and I wouldn't mind coming here again. And since the checkout operator is generally the last person the customer sees, the memory of that transactional interchange can be particularly powerful.

Now read on. There are some stories here which show that many customer service people understand very well what they're *for*. And when you're tired of reading, try asking yourself: "What am I *for*?" I hope you get a worthwhile answer but if you don't, consider what has to change before you do.

Several years ago my family was on holiday in a hotel in Italy. It was a well run hotel, but one incident in particular filled us with delight. The children had taken with them an entire suitcase of cuddly toys. We returned to our room after a day at the beach to find that the cleaners had done something beyond the usual call of duty. They had positioned the animals in a little circle on the bed so that it looked like they were having a meeting. It took a little extra time and effort, but it made our family very happy. The initiative led not only to extra happiness but also to a big tip.

From The Art of Being Kind by Stefan Einhorn (Little, Brown)

On my first day in the Sky sales department, I had to make a call to a potential customer with my managers listening in.

A very elderly lady answered and, because I was so nervous, I found myself saying: "Hello, this is Gabriella calling from the sky" rather than: "This is Gabriella from Sky".

"Ooooh, I'm terribly sorry for not making a donation at church last week," the old dear replied, sounding concerned. "Please don't take it out on Albert."

Readers Digest (but who was Albert?)

Customer service that's customised to the needs of the customer ...

A lady walked into a drug store and told the pharmacist she needed some cyanide.

The pharmacist said: "Why in the world do you need cyanide?"

The lady explained that she needed it to poison her husband.

The pharmacist's eyes opened wide as he said: "Lord have mercy, I can't give you cyanide to kill your husband. That's against the law – I'd lose my licence – they'd throw both of us in jail and all kinds of bad things would happen".

The lady reached into her purse and pulled out a picture of her husband having dinner in a restaurant with the pharmacist's wife.

The pharmacist looked at the picture and replied: "Well, now – you didn't tell me you had a prescription".

I recently shampooed my pet rabbit with Body Shop shampoo. His eyes bulged out and turned red. If you tested your stuff on animals like everyone else, this sort of thing wouldn't happen.

Extract from customer complaint letter to Anita Roddick

The Hawthorne Effect lives on ...

Placebos produce noticeable improvements across a whole range of symptoms and illnesses, such as pain, tiredness, nausea, high blood pressure, angina, asthma, hay fever, headaches, PMT, depression, anxiety, peptic ulcers, high cholesterol, insomnia, hot flushes and social problems. They can reduce the frequency of epileptic seizures, have nasty side effects and reverse the effects of powerful drugs.

Placebos even work if you tell patients that's what they're taking. In one study, 15 psychiatric patients suffering from neurotic symptoms were told: "We feel that a so-called sugar pill may help you.

Do you know what a sugar pill is? A sugar pill is a pill with no medicine in it at all. I think this pill will help you as it has helped so many others. Are you willing to try this pill?"

Fourteen said yes and 13 improved, some a great deal, including one previously suicidal patient.

L. Park and L. Covi, 'Non blind placebo trial'
Archives of General Psychiatry 1965, Vol 12, pp. 336-345

Going the extra mile ...

At the height of the gale, the harbourmaster radioed a coastguard and asked him to estimate the wind speed. He replied he was sorry but he didn't have a gauge. However, if it was any help, the wind had just blown his Land Rover off the cliff.

A young girl who was blown out to sea on a set of inflatable teeth was rescued by a man on an inflatable lobster.

A coastguard spokesman commented: "This sort of thing is all too common".

Early one morning I approached Pret A Manger to buy a coffee. The door was locked as the shop hadn't opened. As I turned to leave, an employee was arriving for work. He asked if it was just coffee I wanted. I said 'Yes', so he offered to pop in and make me one. He reappeared a few minutes later with the coffee. I handed him my £1.60 but he wouldn't accept it. He said if he could start his day by delighting a customer it would make his day a better one. Fantastic! Guess who is now a loyal customer!

Respondent to the ICS Service Reputations Survey, 2003-05

'Every Rectal Thermometer made by Johnson & Johnson is personally tested.'

Product literature

The customer-focused crematorium

Apparently the choice of music for funerals is becoming much more eclectic, e.g. Gracie Fields singing 'Wish me luck as you wave me goodbye' or 'Straight down the middle' sung by Bing Crosby at the funeral of a golfer.

Countdown has made its own contribution. Some time ago the producers had a letter from a lady saying that her grandfather had passed away peacefully while watching Countdown [what a way to go!] and could they please play the 30-second jingle that appears in the programme as the contestants try to think of words or work out their sums? Countdown readily agreed and we like to think that the music was used to accompany the disappearance of the coffin behind the velvet curtains.

I know you want me to go the extra mile, but this is ridiculous

A photo was recently sent to one of the water utility companies, along with the accompanying letter:

This might seem like a strange request but some weeks ago I met a lady who worked in your Customer Services Department. I met her at a dance ... about six weeks ago on a Saturday night. I do not know her name, but she is about 40 years of age, 5 ft 5 in tall, black curly hair and I think she said that she came from Middlesbrough way because she did have a Geordie accent. This lady touched my heart and I would appreciate my photo being passed around in the hope that this lady recognises me. Please call me.

Police in Southampton are handing out free lollipops to late-night revellers in an attempt to reduce violence on the streets. Just one hitch: a fight broke out when one man didn't get one.

I DIDN'T GET MY LOLLIPOP !!!

If you ever wondered what the word 'serendipity' meant...

ukonline.gov.uk is temporarily unavailable. Service will be restored as soon as possible. Apologies for any convenience, please visit the site again soon.

Government website, reported in Private Eye

Sometimes they never know when to stop ...

Customer service can be overdone, as in some luxury hotels that offer that unusual combination, a 'restful atmosphere' plus 'untiring hospitality'. If you have ever stayed in an hotel where you are subjected to the almost constant attentions of a valet, room attendants (i.e. maids), people from housekeeping, waiters who see you as a vehicle for job satisfaction and a break from the tedium of their existence, butlers and cloying receptionists, you will know what I mean. Here is some advice you may find helpful:

• *Lady Celestria Noel, expert on etiquette and author of Debrett's Guide to the Season:* "If you are staying in an hotel with real service, such as a valet, you should try not to be all English and diffident about it. If you have a butler or a maid who is attentive to the point of awkwardness, keep them out of the way by setting them some difficult tasks. They are there to serve you and you should act with due aplomb. You should have no reservations about saying, 'I can't bear the sight of lemon in my water. Please find me some slices of kumquat peel', or, 'I can't abide Veuve Clicquot. Please find me some Pol Roger'."

• *Mary Killen, a social commentator and agony aunt for The Spectator:* "Being in a grand hotel is like being in hospital. It is the one time you just have to sit back and be treated like a halfwit. If people want to pick up your bookmark, you should let them. Most of the staff probably have some pride in their jobs, so to pick it up yourself could be seen as unsporting."

• According to one former butler from the Lanesborough Hotel in London, the most popular guests are often the most demanding ones. "It's the guests who are too self-conscious to ask for their underwear to be washed who tend to leave the measliest tip and command the least respect. There's no stigma about being in service, so a guest should have no reservations about asking for precisely what they want."

Sunday Telegraph, 18 July 2004

We hope you have enjoyed your flight with us. If you have, thank you for choosing EasyJet. If not, then thank you for choosing Ryanair.

Announcement on an EasyJet flight from Zurich to London, just prior to touchdown

Stories about customers and customer service experiences

The Church communicates with its customers ...

- The sermon this morning: "Jesus Walks on Water". The sermon this evening: "Searching for Jesus"

- For those of you who have children and don't know it, we have a nursery downstairs

- The eighth-graders will be presenting Shakespeare's *'Hamlet'* in the church basement on Friday at 7 pm. The congregation is invited to attend this tragedy

- Sunday School: children will be led in sinning and Bible study

- Remember in prayer the many who are sick of our community

- Don't let worry kill you – let the church help

- Say "Hell" to someone who doesn't care much about you

- The ladies of the church have cast off clothing of every kind – they may be seen in the basement on Friday afternoon

- Ladies, don't forget the rummage sale. It's a chance to get rid of those things not worth keeping around the house. Don't forget your husbands

- Next Thursday there will be try-outs for the choir. They need all the help they can get

- Eight new choir robes are currently needed due to the addition of several new members and to the deterioration of some older ones

- Miss Charlene Mason sang 'I will not pass this way again', giving obvious pleasure to the congregation

- Weight Watchers will meet at 7 pm at the First Presbyterian Church. Please use the large double door at the side entrance

- The Low Self-Esteem Support Group will meet on Thursday at 7 pm. Please use the back door

- Scouts are saving aluminium cans, bottles and other items to be recycled. Proceeds will be used to cripple children

- Please place your donation in the envelope along with the deceased person you want remembered

- Attend and you will hear an excellent speaker and heave a healthy lunch

- The associate minister unveiled the church's new tithing campaign slogan last Sunday: 'I Upped my Pledge – Up Yours'.

"The law is perfectly clear," Jerry Jelusich of Multnomah County's Department of Human Services told a press conference in Portland, Oregon. "And it requires us to provide information in all the languages our clients speak. Mental health patients in this county currently speak a total of 55 languages, including some rather unusual ones, and that's why we're advertising a post for an interpreter who is fluent in Klingon."

Jelusich was explaining why Government money was being used to fund a post for a linguist specialising in a fantasy language, invented for the *Star Trek* TV show. "Although it was created by Gene Roddenberry for a work of fiction, the Klingon language was designed from the outset to have a consistent grammar, syntax and vocabulary. And recent research has shown that many people, and not just fans, now regard Klingon as a complete language. Moreover, we've had a growing number of cases involving mental patients where Klingon is the only language they would speak. We need to communicate with them somehow and if hiring a Klingon interpreter enables us to diagnose their problems more effectively, then it's money well spent."

Florida Sun Sentinel, reported in Private Eye

My sister and her husband live in Budapest. They have discovered that the locals possess some peculiar old-fashioned courtesies.

On the day they moved into their new flat, the postman introduced himself and gave them a rough idea of when to expect their mail. He went on to explain that he never delivered bills on a Friday because he couldn't bear the thought of ruining a weekend.

"However," he added, "If you don't think you could face them on a Monday morning either, I don't mind keeping them back until Tuesday".

Magazine letter from reader in Ashton-under-Lyne

Shhh... That's the sound of nobody caring what you think

By Ted Johns

Our very first research report, *The Future of Customer Service* (Institute of Customer Service, 1998), demonstrated that customer service demands had increased dramatically throughout the 1990s. Today, customers demand more access time (often 24/7), are less willing to wait, expect faster responses, want more information, have less patience with broken promises, are more willing to complain and have become both more aggressive and more litigious.

Our *National Complaints Culture Survey 2006* report makes it quite clear that these customer aspirations continue to accelerate:

- Two-thirds of customers expect a person-to-person complaint to be resolved on the same day (compared with 56% in 2001)

- 61% expect a telephone complaint to be resolved on the same day (51% in 2001)

- 95% expect a written complaint at least to be acknowledged and the vast majority want the acknowledgment to be received within a week

- 86% would like a response to a written complaint within 10 working days

- The willingness to complain about products has risen from 50% in 2001 to 60% in 2006 and now exceeds two-thirds of all customers

- One important change is the preference for using the Internet or email as the preferred channel to complain. This has now reached nearly 50% of all customers and the preference for letters has fallen dramatically.

It's worth emphasising that about 90% of customers now say they are more likely to tell others about bad service experiences, though the number talking about good experiences has actually fallen to 60%. Perhaps this is because there are fewer people who can recall ever having had a good service experience, whereas there are

Stories about customers and customer service experiences

plenty who've had bad ones.

What is especially worrying is the gradual growth in the proportion of customers who don't trust what organisations say or do to them, and who (therefore) think it legitimate to act in untrustworthy ways themselves.

Some research suggests that the willingness of customers to act unethically is particularly noticeable among younger consumers. If this is so, and unethical actions are thought to be 'rewarded' (i.e. exaggerated insurance claims lead to superior payouts, clothes worn to a wedding are returned to the retailer for a full refund because they "don't fit", even though there is still confetti in the pockets), then such behaviours become embedded and even transmit themselves into the next generation. Small wonder, then, that some organisations begin to treat customer complaints with suspicion, despite the fact that doing so creates its own customer-initiated backlash.

There is a better way. Sir Terry Leahy, Chief Executive of Tesco, has said that 95% of his customers are honest, dependable, competent and reliable. He does not want to alienate them by burdening them with the types of meticulous scrutiny that might be needed to curb the activities of the other 5% who are dishonest, exploitative, evil and corrupt (my words, not his). If Tesco were to introduce detailed controls in an effort to catch the deviant 5%, they could find that at least some of the other 95%, previously honest and law-abiding, now become truculent and deceitful themselves. And, believe me, if customers want to evade whatever regulations they are meant to absorb, they will always be ingenious enough to do so. That's why Darwin was right when he pointed out that, ultimately, evolution takes care of everything.

The fact is that trust is a reciprocal relationship. If we are to trust the organisations that supply us with things, they have to behave in ways which make it more likely that we can safely trust them. They certainly have no automatic right to be trusted. It follows, by the way, that we customers have no automatic right to be trusted either. It's just that if we don't trust organisations, and they don't trust us, then the relationship soon becomes very complicated, adversarial and hostile, so we all have to start somewhere.

I was at an hotel in the Midlands recently and was intrigued by a badge worn by a member of the hotel's staff. Underneath her name, it said: 'It's with flair that I give customer care'.

I asked her what it was all about.

"Oh, that", she replied. "We've been taken over since then. That offer's finished."

Geoff Burch, speaking at the annual SOCAP UK conference, 2002

Given the things some customers complain about, it's not surprising that complaints get ignored, as these examples from the package holiday business make clear ...

No one told us there would be fish in the sea. The children were startled.

It took us nine hours to fly to Jamaica from England – it only took the Americans three hours.

My fiancé and I booked a twin-bedded room and we were placed in a double-bedded room. We now hold you responsible for the fact that I find myself pregnant. This would not have happened if you had put us in the room we booked.

We found the sand was not like the sand in the brochure. Your brochure shows the sand as yellow but it was white.

We had to queue outside with no air conditioning.

And, from a holidaymaker who'd been to Spain: There were too many Spanish people. The receptionist spoke Spanish. The food is Spanish. Too many foreigners.

Stories about customers and customer service experiences

One of our eagle-eyed newspapers recently reported that someone had spotted a bag in her dustbin. Fortunately she is a conscientious and public-spirited citizen, so she examined the contents in an effort to identify the owner. She found a purse containing some credit cards, a driving licence and even (astonishingly) some cash. Doing what she believed was the honourable thing, our friend the citizen phoned the credit card company's lost-and-found office to pass on the news to the bag owner that her property was safe.

You would think this was a straightforward task and one that might even elicit some gratitude, either from the bag owner or from those lovely people at the credit card company. You might think that but, of course, you would be wrong. The bank's lost-and-found office said it could not pass on the good news because (wait for it) the Data Protection Act doesn't allow interventions of this potentially useful nature to be initiated.

So the citizen agrees to be transferred to another 'helpline' (never has that word been used more inappropriately) which turns out to be an overseas contact centre. She explains the situation all over again. The operator says she can't contact the customer because (a) her job is to cancel cards and (b) contact centres cannot make outward-bound phone calls.

Our friend the citizen – whose citizenship values are by now being tested to their limit – finally gets in touch with the owner of the stolen bag by using the details on her driving licence. That's perhaps what she should have done in the first place – and probably would have done had she known she was going to encounter the full might of the Data Protection Act and somebody who thinks that because her job is to cancel cards then she can't be expected to be interested in any other customer-related problems.

If you sometimes wonder why customers are ignored, it's because the people in the organisation have more than enough to do, as these pieces of 'office wisdom' from *The Office* will testify:

- *Eagles may soar high, but weasels don't get sucked into jet engines*

- *Lack of planning on your part does not constitute an emergency on my part*

- *Process and procedure are the last hiding place of people without the wit and wisdom to do their job properly*

- *Remember that age and treachery will always triumph over youth and ability*

- *Never do today that which will become someone else's responsibility tomorrow*

- *Show me a good loser and I'll show you a LOSER!*

- *Put the key of despair into the lock of apathy. Turn the knob of mediocrity slowly and open the gates of despondency – welcome to a day in the average office*

- *When confronted by a difficult problem, you can solve it more easily by reducing it to the question: "How would the Lone Ranger handle this?"*

- *Accept that some days you are the pigeon and some days you are the statue*

- *If you treat the people around you with love and respect they will never guess that you're trying to get them sacked.*

Commenting on a complaint from a Mr Arthur Purdey about a large gas bill, a spokesman for North West Gas said: "We agree it was rather high for the time of the year. It's possible Mr Purdey has been charged for the gas used up during the explosion that destroyed his house". *Daily Telegraph*

End of the line
It would seem that those who run our railways are even more snowed under than previously thought. A recent telephone call proceeded no further than "Welcome to National Rail Enquiries. Please hang up now".

Letter to The Times

Mrs Irene Graham of Thorpe Avenue, Boscombe, delighted the audience with her reminiscences of the German prisoner of war who was sent each week to do her garden. He was repatriated at the end of 1945. She recalled: "He'd always seemed a nice, friendly chap but when the crocuses came up in the middle of our lawn in February 1946, they spelt out 'Heil Hitler'".

Bournemouth Evening Echo

IF YOU'D LIKE TO HEAR ALL OF YOUR OPTIONS AGAIN, PRESS 49. IF YOU'VE FORGOTTEN WHY YOU CALLED IN THE FIRST PLACE, PRESS 50.

By Ted Johns

Letter of apology from a train operating company to a disgruntled passenger who had found a flea on his carriage seat:

Dear Sir

I cannot begin to describe my embarrassment, shame and deep regret on hearing of your most unfortunate experience recently on one of our train services.

This must have been truly awful for you. Both I and my colleagues are appalled that you should have had to go through this dreadful (and, I might add, quite exceptional) experience. Please accept my most sincere apologies on behalf of the firm, a voucher for a free journey of your choosing and the promise, and commitment, that nothing like this will ever happen to you again as a valued customer of our company.

On the reverse side of the paper was a Post-it Note bearing the handwritten words: "Jane, send this guy the bug letter".

**Flight announcement on SouthWest Airlines –
from the Cabin Services Director:**

"Welcome to SouthWest Airlines. Pick up your seatbelt, insert the metal
tab into the buckle and pull tight. It works just like any other seat belt and if
you don't know how to operate one, you probably shouldn't be out in
public unsupervised.

In the event of a sudden loss of cabin pressure, oxygen masks will descend
from the ceiling. Stop screaming, grab the mask and pull it over your face. If
you have a small child travelling with you, secure your mask before assisting
with theirs. If you are travelling with two small children, decide which one you
love more.

Weather at our destination is 50 degrees with some broken clouds, but they'll
try to have them fixed before we arrive.

Thank you and, remember, nobody loves you or your money more than
SouthWest Airlines."

**Flight announcement on SouthWest Airlines –
from the Captain:**

"Ladies and gentlemen, we are pleased to have some of the best flight
attendants in the industry. Unfortunately none of them are on this flight ..."

AT THIS TIME, WE'D LIKE TO REMIND YOU
TO EAT AND DRINK AT REGULAR INTERVALS.
THANK YOU FOR CONTINUING TO HOLD.

Helpful suggestion often found on the notice-board in call centres

Window of opportunity

At Liverpool Football Club, they have a system called PTS – Priority Ticket Scheme – which, for about £50 a year, enables fans to phone and buy tickets before they go on general sale.

One fan duly attempted to ring on a Monday to obtain tickets for an Everton derby match but gave up, frustrated, after more than four hours and decided to go to the Anfield ticket office the next day. This is how the conversation at the ticket-office window went.

Fan: Got any tickets left for Everton?

Official: Yes, quite a few.

Fan: Can I have one? I'm on the PTS.

Official: No, they are only on sale by phone.

Fan: But I tried doing that for four hours yesterday.

Official: You couldn't have. But anyway, I can only sell you one if you phone up. [At this point, the fan takes out his mobile phone and rings the office number. The phone beside the official rings.]

Official: Good morning, Liverpool Football Club here. How may I help you?

Fan: Yes, it's me at the window. Can I have an Everton ticket, please?

Official: Yes, sir. What's your PTS number?

Fan: Here. [He holds up his card to the window for the official to see.]

Official: And how will you be paying, sir?

Fan: Credit card.

Official: And the number? [The fan holds up the credit card to the window.]

Official: OK. Your ticket will be in the post.

Fan: Can't you just give it me here to save on the postage?

Official: No, sir. I'm not allowed to do that. [Official puts the phone down and smiles at the fan. The ticket arrived in the post the next morning.]

> When I hear about people making vast fortunes without doing any productive work or contributing anything to society, my reaction is, 'How do I get in on that?'
>
> *Dave Barry*

> The quietest place in the world is the complaints department at the parachute packing plant.
>
> *Jackie Martling*

There must be a saying that pervades many businesses in their quest for the easy way out: "The job is not done until you have come up with a really good reason as to why the job is not done". To help you in this search, here are 101 of the world's favourite excuses, listed in alphabetical order. Using this framework, you can simply quote numbers in future and thus avoid the necessity of actually spelling out the excuse when you need one.

Our source for this brilliant innovation is Timothy R.V. Foster's book, *101 Ways to Boost Customer Satisfaction* (Kogan Page).

1. Accident
2. Air traffic control delays
3. Alarm didn't go off
4. Answerphone not working
5. Arrested
6. Battery ran flat
7. Bomb scare/security alert
8. Burglary/theft
9. Can't find file on hard disk
10. Car broke down
11. Car stolen/vandalised
12. Cheque is in the post
13. Computer crashed
14. Computers are down
15. Couldn't concentrate
16. Decision-maker on holiday
17. Dependant accident/sick
18. Did it wrong
19. Didn't feel like it
20. Didn't feel well
21. Didn't get round to it
22. Didn't have the materials
23. Didn't notice the time
24. Didn't know it was holiday
25. Didn't see the message
26. Didn't understand
27. Died
28. Disk crashed
29. Drunk
30. Earthquake
31. Electricity cut
32. Fax paper ran out
33. Fax unreadable/garbled
34. Fire
35. Flat tyre
36. Flood
37. Forgot keys
38. Forgot to do it
39. Funding didn't come through
40. Genuine mistake
41. Got into a loop
42. Got out at wrong station
43. Had a heart attack
44. Had the wrong materials
45. Had to take a phone call
46. Hasn't returned my call
47. Hung-over
48. In jail
49. Insurance ran out
50. Invoice not approved
51. Left a page in photocopier
52. Left ticket/passport behind
53. Locked out
54. Lost in the post
55. Lost my passport
56. Lost my ticket
57. Lost the disk
58. Misfiled
59. Missed the bus/train/plane
60. New baby
61. No budget
62. Nobody to sign the cheque
63. Not enough time
64. Not insured
65. Not on strategy
66. Not top priority
67. Over budget
68. Pilot error
69. Playing telephone tag
70. Pressed wrong button
71. Project not approved
72. Proposal rejected
73. Ran out of materials
74. Relative/colleague died
75. Robbery/mugging
76. Same case
77. Same name
78. Someone took it by mistake
79. Something else came up
80. Stopped for speeding
81. Storm
82. Strike
83. Supplier late
84. There's a lot of it about
85. Too busy
86. Too cold/hot
87. Too dark/light
88. Took wrong bus/train/plane
89. Took wrong turning
90. Traffic jam/diversion
91. Train broke down
92. Train late
93. Upset stomach/flu/cold
94. War
95. Wrong address
96. Wrong computer system
97. Wrong fax number
98. Wrong materials
99. Wrong spelling
100. Wrong phone number
101. Wrong time zone

Significant signs sometimes seen in call centres and other places where concern for the customer is meant to be uppermost in the minds of everyone who works there

Rome did not create a great empire by having meetings, they did it by killing all those who opposed them

Doing the job RIGHT the first time gets the job done.
Doing the job WRONG 14 times gives you job security

Artificial Intelligence is no match for Natural Stupidity

If at first you don't succeed – try management

Never put off until tomorrow what you can avoid altogether

TEAMWORK – means never having to take all the blame yourself

The beatings will continue until morale improves

We waste time, so you don't have to

Hang in there, retirement is only 50 years away

Go the extra mile – it makes your boss look like an incompetent slacker

INDECISION is the key to FLEXIBILITY

Aim low, reach your goals, avoid disappointment

We waste more time by 8 o'clock in the morning than other companies do all day

You pretend to work and we'll pretend to pay you

Stories about customers and customer service experiences

Don't make me use upper case - the customer bites back

By Ted Johns

The other day I wanted some euros. On my wife's advice, I went into our local branch of her bank. The man behind the counter used to be what they called a 'cashier' but now he is a 'Jack' (of all trades). I asked him whether I could buy some euros even though I am not one of his bank's customers.

"Yes sir," he said. This was a promising start. It suggested a desire to help ("yes") plus an appropriately deferential attitude ("sir").

For me there were only two further questions. First, how many euros did I want? (Answer: 420.) Second, how did I want to pay? (Answer: Mastercard.)

I now expected the transaction to proceed. If so, I was naive beyond belief. "I just need to take a few details," says my friend Jack, pulling a four-page application form towards him. "First, can I have your name, address and date of birth? And have you got some form of photographic ID with you, like a driving licence or your passport?"

Whoa. Stop right there. I want €420. I am not a money-launderer or a drug-dealer, nor do I look like a money-launderer or a drug-dealer: "Yes, well, sir, they're the worst, you see, the ones who don't look like they're drug-dealers; we always scrutinise them much more carefully because people who look honest almost invariably aren't".

Why do they want my date of birth? And why must I prove who I am? I want €420. The Bank of England is not going to be quaking in its boots.

Of course, the answer is that they don't have to get all these 'few details'. There are really three reasons why my new friend Jack is engaging in this rigmarole. None of them is anything to do with money-laundering or drug dealing.

First, the bank has its 'procedures'. These have been created without any regard for their concern about the customer's sensitivities. Remember: I am not a customer of this bank but I am now on their premises, I have been enticed inside, so they now have the opportunity to turn me into one of their customers. As it is I shall never darken their doorway again.

The rationale for the bank's 'procedures' is that they reflect a legal obligation (they don't) and because they are Financial

Services Authority requirements (they aren't). Note that the customer is expected to comply with these 'procedures', while the bank absolves itself of any responsibility for them. It's important to note that there isn't just a single 'procedure' for all the banks, but a separate set for each one. This tells us straightaway that these 'procedures' aren't a product of some centrally-imposed legislation or regulatory diktat.

Second, the 'procedures' developed within this bank are the outcome from some viciously internecine negotiations, with every bank function wishing to establish its 'right' to control the 'procedures' while vigorously resisting the claims of others. The result is a set of 'procedures' that attempts to balance the concerns of all the interested stakeholders. These stakeholders do not include the customer.

Third, the bank wants to add me to their database of likely prospects. Who knows, perhaps my name will help Jack to achieve his monthly targets and therefore keep his job a little while longer. Personally, I am not much interested in whether he keeps his job or loses it and I certainly don't want to be a pawn in his career ambitions, a mere Sherpa helping him to climb up the greasy corporate ladder.

I retrieve my credit card (which, by the way, has already been suspiciously scrutinised on both sides) and sashay down to our village Post Office, which sells me €420 there and then, no questions asked. As I depart, I am encouraged to have a nice day. For the bank, another sale is lost, another potential customer disappears.

We are all the victims of 'procedures', rules and regulations that are increasingly oppressive and restrictive, yet driven by an 'industry' of people whose whole livelihoods depend on (a) creating interventionist rules, (b) implementing them, (c) enforcing them and (d) making them even more impenetrable.

Yet until recently, we customers weren't treated as idiots. If anything, the authors of product instructions often made exaggerated assumptions about our intelligence and wrote as if all customers are:

- well-behaved, systematic and anally retentive

- sensible, thoughtful, phlegmatic and not prone to bursts of over-excitement or vicious temper

- literate, especially when reading material that has been imperfectly translated from the Koran

- sober or teetotal

- of average height and weight
- fit, athletic, mobile and healthy
- equipped with a good working knowledge of elementary physics, chemistry, electrical and mechanical engineering
- capable of translating a two-dimensional diagram into a three-dimensional reality
- familiar with not just the principles but also the most modern applications of information technology
- able to suppress any impulses towards unconventional behaviour
- prepared to read instructions before taking action, as opposed to attempting action first and then only reading the instructions as a form of problem-solving backstop once the camera has blown up or the self-assembly wardrobe collapsed into pieces.

It has taken many years for companies to appreciate that some of their customers aren't all these things and a few aren't any of them. Yet these same customers have money and so far most organisations have baulked at suggesting that prospective purchasers must pass an intelligence, spatial ability and mechanical aptitude test before being allowed to buy their products.

The only alternative has been to make product instructions as idiot-proof as possible, even though this is a goal which is physically unattainable, simply because there is always an idiot, somewhere, who can act more idiotically than you could ever imagine.

So why don't we think laterally and abandon rules, regulations and product instructions altogether?

Drachten, a town in northern Holland, led by the inspired Hans Monderman, in charge of traffic planning, took all its traffic lights and road signs away in 1999. Immediately, motorists started to drive more carefully. *Because they were thinking about the possibility of fatal accidents, they didn't have any*. Since 1999 Drachten has had no highway deaths – and it doesn't have any tailbacks either.

Essentially, there are two approaches to rule-making in society so far as we customers are concerned:

1. *You can attempt to create rules for every situation*

2. *You can set a framework within which people can make informed choices.*

Rules for every situation work best when:

- the objectives of the rule (and the product instruction) are obvious

- it is reasonably easy whether or not the rule has been obeyed and implemented

- the content and the purpose of the rule are not likely to change over time.

Examples include rules about the release of harmful smoke emissions into the atmosphere, the avoidance of food with poisonous substances and the desirability of keeping clients' money in a separate account.

On the other hand, general principles which leave it to the customer's discretion about the degree of risk they are prepared to take are more sensible:

- When the situation is more complex, e.g. when the customer, with his own special financial circumstances, is buying an investment service or product

- When the application of the rules requires a degree of knowledge about the customer which the rule-maker doesn't have

- When observance of the rule is more difficult to monitor

- When the rule book changes frequently.

Rick Haythornwaite, Chairman of the Better Regulation Commission, has pointed out:

"Our national resilience, self-reliance and spirit of adventure could be threatened by a culture that demands the progressive elimination of risk through more and more regulation".

As in all of life's colourful dimensions, including alcohol and chocolate, there should be moderation in all things. In this chapter, as in some of the other chapters in this book, you can read about what happens when people forget this elementary principle.

US rules on the use of respirators at work

Paragraph (g)(1)(i)(A) of the US Government's Occupational Safety and Health Administration's rules on respirators prohibits the use of respirators for employees with "facial hair that comes between the sealing surface of the face piece and the face". In case you're wondering what this means, if you have a beard then you mustn't use a normal respirator because it won't work properly.

Faced with the possibility that people can equip themselves with an enormous range of beards, not to mention designer stubble, the Occupational Safety and Health Administration has created a galaxy of rules governing the actions to take for employees with various types, sizes, curliness and textures of beards.

This is alleged to be an actual letter sent to one of the High Street banks, whose manager thought it amusing enough to have it published in *The Guardian*.

Dear Sir

I am writing to thank you for bouncing my cheque with which I endeavoured to pay my plumber last month. By my calculations some three nanoseconds must have elapsed between his presenting the cheque and the arrival in my account of the funds needed to honour it. I refer, of course, to the automatic monthly deposit of my entire salary, an arrangement which, I admit, has only been in place for eight years.

You are to be commended for seizing that brief window of opportunity and also for debiting £50 from my account by way of penalty for the inconvenience I caused to your bank. My thankfulness springs from the manner in which this incident has caused me to rethink my errant financial ways.

You have set me on the path of fiscal righteousness. No more will our relationship be blighted by these unpleasant incidents, for I am restructuring my affairs, taking as my model the procedures, attitudes and conduct of your very bank. I can think of no greater compliment and I know you will be excited and proud to hear it. To this end, please be advised about the following changes.

I have noticed that whereas I personally attend to your telephone calls and letters, when I try to contact you I am confronted by the impersonal, ever-changing pre-recorded, faceless entity which your bank has become. From now on I, like you, choose only to deal with a flesh-and-blood person. My mortgage and loan repayments will, therefore and hereafter, no longer be automatic, but will arrive at your bank, by cheque, addressed personally and confidentially to an employee at your branch whom you must nominate. You will be aware that it is an offence under the Postal Act for any other person to open such an envelope.

Please find attached an Application Contact Status form which I require your chosen employee to complete. I am sorry it runs to eight pages, but in order that I know as much about him or her as your bank knows about me, there is no alternative.

Please note that all copies of his or her medical history must be countersigned by a Notary Public and the mandatory details of his/her financial situation (income, debts, assets and liabilities) must be accompanied by documented proof.

In due course I will issue your employee with a PIN number which he/she must quote in dealings with me. I regret that it cannot be shorter than 28 digits but, again, I have modelled it on the number of button presses required to access my account balance on your phone bank service.

As they say, imitation is the sincerest form of flattery. Let me level the playing field even further by introducing you to my new telephone system which, you will notice, is very much like yours. My Authorised Contact at your bank, the only person with whom I will have any dealings, may call me at any time and will be answered by an automated voice service:

Press buttons as follows:

1 To make an appointment to see me
2 To query a missing payment
3 To transfer the call to my living room in case I am there
4 To transfer the call to my bedroom in case I am sleeping
5 To transfer the call to my toilet in case I am attending to nature
6 To transfer the call to my mobile phone if I am not at home
7 To leave a message on my computer, a password to access my computer is required. The password will be communicated at a later date to the Authorised Contact
8 To return to the main menu and to listen to options 1 through 9
9 To make a general complaint or inquiry. The contact will then be put on hold, pending the attention of my automated answering service.

While this may on occasions involve a lengthy wait, uplifting music will play for the duration of the call. This month I've chosen a refrain from 'The Best of Woodie Guthrie':

"Oh, the banks are made of marble,
With a guard on every door,
And the vaults are filled with silver,
That the miners sweated for".

On a more serious note, we come to the matter of cost. As your bank has often pointed out, the ongoing drive for greater efficiency comes at a cost which you have always been quick to pass on to me. Let me repay your kindness by passing some costs back. First, there is the matter of the advertising material you send me. This I will read for a fee of £20 per page. Enquiries from the Authorised Contact will be billed at £5 per minute of my time spent in response.

Any debits to my account as, for example, in the matter of the penalty for the dishonoured cheque, will be passed back to you. My new phone service runs at 75p a minute. You will be well advised to keep your Enquiries brief and to the point.

Regrettably, but again following your example, I must also levy an establishment fee to cover the setting up of this new arrangement.

Your Humble Client [name withheld]

No one decides to be a comedian. It's the audience that decides.

Eric Sykes, who clearly knows a thing or two about the power of the customer

A woman called a local hospital. "Hello, could you connect me to the person who gives information about patients? I'd like to find out if a family member is doing better."

The voice at the other end said: "What is the patient's name and room number?"

"Sarah Finkel, Room 302."

"I'll connect you to the nursing station."

"3-A Nursing Station. How can I help you?"

"I'd like to know the condition of Sarah Finkel in Room 302."

"Are you a family member?"

"Yes, yes I am."

"Hold on – let me look at her records. Yes, Mrs Finkel is doing very well. In fact she's had two full meals, her blood pressure is fine, she is to be taken off the heart monitor in a couple of hours and, if she continues this improvement, it looks like Dr Cohen is going to send her home very soon."

"What a relief! Oh, that's fantastic – that's wonderful news!"

The nurse said: "From your enthusiasm, I take it you are a sister or perhaps an aunt?"

"Neither, I'm Sarah Finkel in 302 – and nobody ever tells me shit!"

**I went to a restaurant that serves 'breakfast at any time'.
So I ordered French toast during the Renaissance.**

Peter Kay

Mahatma Gandhi is alive and well.

Members of the public in the USA have learned how to jam the phone lines of telemarketers, those infuriating people who interrupt dinner to ask if you have life insurance and whether you want your double-glazing renewed. The American Teleservices Association, as a result, has been forced to change its phone number and has complained about being pestered.

The act of communal mischief began when Dave Barry, a syndicated columnist in the USA, suggested that readers call the ATA. "Tell them what you think!" he wrote. "Be sure to wipe your mouthpiece afterwards."

Thousands of calls, many of them highly abusive, swamped the ATA switchboard, which gave up answering the phone and instead played a recorded message: "We are sorry, you have reached a number that has been disconnected".

The telemarketing industry in the USA was already under pressure from the introduction of a national 'Do Not Call Registry', which imposes severe penalties on companies caught making sales calls to those who have signed up to the list.

The ATA has warned that "millions" of jobs are at risk from the new rules. Mr Barry wrote: "You could use pretty much the same reasoning to argue that laws against mugging cause unemployment among muggers".

The industry is failing to see the joke. ATA Executive Director Tim Searcy said: "It's difficult not to see some malice in Mr Barry's intent".

Mr Barry responded: "I feel just terrible, especially if they were eating or anything".

Customer 1, Ryanair nil

My affections for Ryanair, with its thrilling disregard for whingeing passengers, vary according to mood and circumstance. But both conspired against the airline on Monday night at Girona airport in Spain. I was tired, it was late and I was anxious about getting back to London from Luton at midnight. So I opted to take hand luggage only.

There was only one problem. "Your bag weighs almost 12 kilos," the Ryanair desk-person told me. "The limit is 10. You must check it in."

"No, I'll take some things out," I said.

"Then you'll have to throw them away. There are some bins here."

A red mist enveloped me. I looked around at other intending passengers, mountains of wobbly flesh, twice my weight, poised to spill over into my aircraft seat after we boarded. Were they being asked to check in their bellies or their buttocks?

"No, I won't," I said, re-opening my case. "I'll wear the extra weight."

"Please stand aside. You're getting in the way of the other passengers."

I stood aside. Then I got down on the floor, emptying the whole case on to the marble. I redressed. I swapped my lightweight shoes for the walking boots I'd packed. I put on waterproof over-trousers over my trousers and a belt, then a huge, thick, gaily-patterned, almost knee-length jersey over my shirt, then a green body warmer over the jersey, then a big down jacket over the body warmer, then an outsize yellow Gore-Tex cagoule (with a hood) over the lot. Also a green scarf.

Then I filled the four capacious net pockets of the cagoule with a DVD, two books, my toilet bag, three handkerchiefs and the chargers for my mobile phone and laptop. Triumphantly I waddled back to the queue (which had been much entertained by the

performance) looking like one of those police-dog trainers swathed in bite-proof clothing. Though I still did not weigh as much as most of the other passengers, my suitcase had shed three kilos. Grinding their teeth, the staff let me through.

The security scan after passport control was quite a trial, but after this I was able to undress again, stuff everything back into the case (they daren't impose weight limits after the boarding gate (or the duty-free rip-off shops would have to close down) and board the flight.

At Luton I swanned past everyone waiting at the carousels and caught, by minutes, the 00.07 train to London Blackfriars. Reader, you can have no idea of the joy this whole episode has afforded your childish columnist. Delicious.

Matthew Parris, The Times, London, 25 January 2007
© NI Syndication, London

If you're worried there aren't enough policemen on the beat ...

Going to bed the other night, I noticed people in my shed stealing things.

I phoned the police but was told no one was in the area to help. They said they would send someone over as soon as possible.

I hung up. A minute later I rang again. "Hello," I said. "I called you a minute ago because there were people in my shed. You don't have to hurry now because I've shot them."

Within minutes there were half a dozen police cars in the area, plus helicopters and an armed response unit. They caught the burglars red-handed.

One of the officers said: "I thought you said you'd shot them".

To which I replied: "I thought you said there was no-one available".

Letter in the Evening Standard

Is this hole one of yours?

The following email was received by one of our more well-known utility companies.

We hope you can shed some light on a hole that has appeared at the rear of our premises and has been motionless ever since.

We have reason to believe it may be one of yours and wondered if you had missed it. We, and our neighbours, do not own any holes and thought it may have dropped off one of your vans by mistake. We would hate to think you might be driving round looking for it, when it is here all the time.

Some of our staff have grown quite attached to the aforesaid hole, even nicknaming it 'Hal'. We reluctantly had to abandon the formal naming ceremony when it was pointed out to us that 'Hal Hole' is a description that could reasonably be applied to a large part of our town.

To prevent it being stolen we thought we could put a sign up claiming it as 'Ours'. However, someone pointed out that we couldn't very well call it 'Ours Hole'.

So all in all, we wondered whether you might like it back?

Now it's
our turn:
if there's a
tourist season,
how come we
can't shoot
them?

By Ted Johns

'Coarse' customer service does not signify something crude, revolting and unpleasant, such as eating mashed potatoes with your fingers, making rude gestures at other drivers or checking your fingernails while a customer is sobbing her heart out in front of you.

According to Michael Green, the author of books about 'coarse' sailing, acting, rugby and drinking, the adjective 'coarse', applied to anything, is "the way things get done in real life, as opposed to the lofty theoretical manner laid down by the authorities". So a Coarse Sailor is one who, in a crisis, forgets all that stuff about port and starboard, but simply shouts: "For God's sake turn left, you fool!" A Coarse Actor is one who always knows the last play better than the one he's actually in. Coarse Rugby is a game played by fewer than 15 people a side, at least half of whom are totally unfit, and a Coarse Drinker is one who blames his hangover on the tonic and not the gin.

So 'coarse' customer service is delivered by people and organisations whose actions may be prompted by the highest possible motives, but whose behaviour is totally ill-matched to the needs and expectations of the customer.

Coarse Customer Service (let's give it some capital letters, as it is a dignified concept) is rarely malevolent.

Some of it occurs because the Coarse Customer Service person, who never wanted to have anything to do with customers in the first place, has an unreasonable addiction to the truth rather than to the on-message corporate spin which he or she should be spouting. In this sense, Coarse Customer Service represents nothing more than the customer-facing person's unconscious desire to establish some personal control over events.

Some of it happens because the Coarse Customer Service person has been wrongly recruited and selected or because the employer thinks that customer service is so straightforward that anybody can do it – which amounts to the same thing.

Let's face it, Coarse Customer Service happens because customers can be very difficult. If you've already had a hard day, you don't particularly like what you're doing, you don't like your manager and you already have some other personal problems (which to you are a good deal more earth-shattering than the comparatively trivial complaints coming at you from the customer), then it wouldn't be surprising if occasionally you lost it.

And if some people sometimes deliver customer service that is 'coarse', whose fault is that? It's certainly too easy to blame them or to blame the customer. The problem *always* lies with the organisation – and the solution *always* lies with the organisation as well:

- All its customer-facing staff must be properly recruited and selected with priority being given to possession of the right attitudes, such as an affinity for people

- The whole corporate culture must be focused on service performance, service improvement and service excellence

- A service ethic must equally be applied to those in back-office and support functions

- Customer service jobs must be designed so that the people doing them are excited, energised and enthused. This means giving people lots of autonomy so that they can operate as a one-stop customer service shop. It means recognising and celebrating service achievement. It means a performance feedback system based on rewarding success rather than penalising failure

- Customers themselves must be educated. If customer problems and information requests are taken seriously and resolved quickly, then customers will have no cause to lose their tempers or become violent.

Put brutally, businesses have two choices. They can work hard at getting more or work hard at getting good. More in the short-term almost always means worse; good in the longer-term almost always means more.

Read these stories and make up your own mind about whether getting more or getting good is the right strategy to follow.

Telephonists are told to remember that a car is often the caller's most treasured possession. This became perfectly clear when one motorist called in to report that his roof had been badly damaged. The interview and form-filling carried on normally for about five minutes until the caller was asked to explain how the damage was caused. It was then he said that somebody had had the poor taste to leap on to his car from a tall building while attempting to commit suicide.

According to The Guardian, more than 40 workers were made redundant at a large telecoms company's call centre when a message flashed on their screens saying: "Please log off your computer and clear your desk".

In 2004, **BBC News** reported that an official in one of Finland's tax offices had died at his desk, but his death was not noticed for two days.

The organisation's Human Resources department later promised that "procedures will have to be reviewed".

What 'procedures'? The procedures for testing that employees are still alive at the end of the working day?

Some apparently genuine messages from London Underground train drivers:

"I am sorry about the delay: apparently some nutter has just wandered into the tunnel at Euston. We don't know when we'll be moving again but these people tend to come out pretty quickly, usually in bits."

"To the gentleman wearing the long grey coat trying to get on the second carriage: what part of 'stand clear of the doors' don't you understand?"

"We are now travelling through Baker Street. As you can see, Baker Street is closed. It would have been nice if they had actually told me so I could tell you earlier, but no, they don't think about things like that."

"Please allow the doors to close. Try not to confuse this with 'Please hold the doors open'. The two are distinct and separate instructions."

"Ladies and gentlemen, I do apologise for the delay to your service. I know you're all dying to get home, unless, of course, you happen to be married to my ex-wife, in which case you'll want to cross over to the Westbound and go in the opposite direction."

By Ted Johns

Final, exasperated words from a call centre agent when closing a service transaction:

"I said, 'Have a nice day', you deaf old cow!"

We once went to St Neots by train. The station is about three miles from the town centre, so I said to the ticket collector: "Why didn't you build the station nearer to the town?"

He looked at me for a long minute (he closely resembled the man in the science fiction film who's the first to see the creature), then said: "We did think about that but in the end we decided it was better to have the station nearer the railway".

A (former) customer of Asda tells us of her encounter with an unusually surly checkout operator. As the transaction drew silently to its close, the customer asked: "Aren't you going to say 'thank you', then?"

The checkout operator smiled – and it was a smile of victory, not a smile of friendship. "No," she said. "We don't have to do that any more because it's printed on the till receipt."

A visiting Health and Safety inspector recently castigated the owner of a Welsh café because one of the waitresses had been "looking at the customers when she was speaking to them". Apparently she should have been looking at the floor, otherwise "when she speaks she may be spraying germs in the customers' faces".

We're up to here with you lot – extracts from police car conversations with sometimes aggressive citizens:

"Yes, sir, you can talk to the shift supervisor but I don't think it will help. Oh, did I mention that I am the shift supervisor?"

"The answer to this last question will determine whether you are drunk or not. Was Mickey Mouse a cat or a dog?"

"Yeah, we have a quota. Two more tickets and my wife gets a toaster."

"You didn't think we give pretty women tickets? You're right, we don't. Sign here."

I recently dialled one of the new directory enquiry numbers at 3 am, after a wedding reception, for the number of a taxi service to pick me up from the hotel and take me home. The operator insisted on putting me straight through. After waiting a couple of rings I was greeted by a very grumpy-sounding lady who was outraged at my request to be picked up from the hotel. When she eventually stopped shouting, I found that her husband was a taxidermist.

Letter in The Daily Telegraph

This is the message that staff at the Pacific Palisades High School in California voted unanimously should be recorded on their telephone answering machine. It came about because the school had implemented a policy requiring students and parents to be responsible for their children's absences and missing homework. The school and teachers are being sued by parents who want their children's fail grades changed to passes, even though the majority of these children were absent between 15 and 30 times during the semester and did not complete enough schoolwork to enable them to accumulate sufficient marks:

Hello! You have reached the automated answering service of the Pacific Palisades High School. In order to assist you in connecting to the right staff member, please listen to all the options before making a selection.

- *To lie about why your child is absent – Press 1*
- *To make excuses for why your child did not do his work – Press 2*
- *To complain about what we do – Press 3*
- *To swear at staff members – Press 4*
- *To ask why you didn't get information that was already enclosed in your newsletter and several flyers mailed to you – Press 5*
- *If you want us to raise your child – Press 6*
- *If you want to reach out and touch, slap or hit someone – Press 7*
- *To request another teacher, for the third time this year – Press 8*
- *To complain about bus transportation – Press 9*
- *To complain about the school lunches – Press 0.*

I was in the express ('six items only') lane at the supermarket, quietly fuming. Completely ignoring the sign, the woman ahead of me had slipped into the checkout queue pushing a trolley piled high with groceries. Imagine my delight when the checkout operator beckoned the woman to come forward, looked into the trolley and asked sweetly: "So which six items would you like to buy?" Wouldn't it be great if that happened more often?

A flight attendant was stationed at the departure gate to check tickets. As a man approached, she extended her hand for the ticket and he opened his trench coat and flashed her. Without missing a beat she said: "Sir, I need to see your ticket, not your stub".

A lady was picking through the frozen turkeys at the supermarket, but couldn't find one big enough for her family. She asked one of the shelf stackers: "Do these turkeys get any bigger?"

"No ma'am," he replied. "They're dead."

The cop got out of his car and the kid who was stopped for speeding rolled down his window. "I've been waiting for you all day," the cop said. The kid replied: "Yeah, well, I got here as fast as I could".

A crowded United Airlines flight had been cancelled and a single agent was rebooking a long line of inconvenienced travellers. Suddenly an angry customer pushed his way to the desk, slapped his ticket down on the counter and shouted: "I HAVE to be on this flight and it has to be FIRST CLASS".

The agent replied: "I'm sorry, sir. I'll be happy to try to help you, but I've got to help these folks first and I'm sure we'll be able to work something out".

The passenger was unimpressed. He asked loudly, so that the passengers behind could hear: "Do you have any idea who I am?"

Without hesitating, the agent smiled and grabbed her public address microphone. "May I have your attention please", she began, her voice clearly audible throughout the terminal. "We have a passenger here at Gate 14 who does not know who he is. If anyone can help him find his identity, please come to Gate 14."

With the people in the queue laughing hysterically, the man glared at the United Airlines' agent, gritted his teeth and swore: "F*** you!"

Without flinching, the agent smiled (again!) and said: "I'm sorry, sir, but you'll have to get in line for that, too!"

A very unattractive and unpleasant woman walks into Wal-Mart with her two children. After shoving her way past several customers waiting to get trolleys, she says to the Wal-Mart greeter: "Go through those trolleys and find me one that doesn't need oiling for once!"

"Yes, ma'am, happy to oblige," says the greeter. "Here you are, ma'am, hope this one is okay."

"If you'd get out of the way, maybe I could find out!" snaps the woman.

"Sorry, ma'am," the greeter says, standing aside, "And you and the twins have a nice day".

The woman snarls: "They're not twins, you moron. They don't even look alike".

The greeter smiles. "No, they don't, ma'am, you're absolutely right. But I just couldn't believe you got laid twice."

PLEASE DON'T THROW YOUR CIGARETTE ENDS ON THE FLOOR. THE COCKROACHES ARE GETTING CANCER.

PLEASE BE SAFE
Do not stand, sit, climb or lean on zoo fences.
If you fall, animals could eat you and that might make them sick.
Thank you.

A man who stole a skull from a Thai museum told police he took it to improve his luck. He said customers who owed him money suddenly started settling their debts.

SINGLE BLACK FEMALE seeks male companionship, ethnicity unimportant. I'm a very good-looking girl who LOVES to play. I love long walks in the woods, riding in your pickup truck, hunting, camping and fishing trips, cozy winter nights lying by the fire. Candlelight dinners will have me eating out of your hand. Rub me the right way and watch me respond. I'll be at the front door when you get home from work, wearing only what nature gave me. Kiss me and I'm yours. Call (404)875-6420 and ask for Daisy.

Personal advertisement in The Atlanta Journal. Over 15,000 men found themselves talking to the Atlanta Humane Society about an eight-week-old black Labrador retriever.

There are teachers and there are educators ...

According to a news report, a certain school in Streatham, south London, was recently faced with a unique problem. A number of girls were beginning to use lipstick and would put it on in the school toilets. That was fine, but after they put on their lipstick they would press their lips to the mirror, leaving dozens of little lip prints. Every night the school's maintenance man would remove them and the next day the girls would put them back.

Finally, the head teacher decided that something had to be done. So she called a number of the girls to the toilets and met them there with the maintenance man. She explained that all these lip prints were causing a major problem for the custodian who had to clean the mirrors every night.

To demonstrate how difficult it was to clean the mirrors, she asked the maintenance man to show the girls how he did it. He took out a long-handled squeegee, dipped it in one of the toilets and cleaned the mirror with it.

Since then, there have been no lip prints on the mirror.

Because of recent disruption on the railways, I asked: "Are the trains running as normal today?" when I bought my ticket.

The ticket clerk looked at me for a moment and then said: "No mate, it's better than that – they're on time."

After a lengthy session with a customer who had been having difficulties with a computer programme, a support technician at my brother's company turned in his report: "The problem resides between the keyboard and the chair".

Late one night I stopped at one of those 24-hour petrol station shops to get myself a freshly brewed cup of coffee.

When I picked up the pot, I noticed that the brew was as black as Tarmac and just about as thick.

"How old is this coffee?" I asked the woman who was standing behind the counter.

She shrugged. "I don't know. I've only been working here two weeks."

The internal customers get on your nerves as well

After every flight, Qantas pilots fill out a form, called a 'gripe sheet', that tells mechanics about problems with the aircraft. The mechanics correct the problems, document their repairs on the form and then the pilots review the gripe sheets before the plane takes to the air again.

Never let it be said that ground crews lack a sense of humour. Here are some actual maintenance complaints submitted by Qantas pilots and the solutions presented by the airline's maintenance engineers.

By the way, Qantas is one of the few, if not the only major airline that has never, ever, had an accident.

Pilot: Left inside main tyre almost needs replacement.
Maintenance: Almost replaced left inside main tyre.

P: Something loose in cockpit.
M: Something tightened in cockpit.

P: Dead bugs on windshield.
M: Live bugs on back order.

P: Evidence of leak on right main landing gear.
M: Evidence removed.

P: DME volume unbelievably loud.
M: DME volume set to more believable level.

P: IFF inoperative in OFF mode.
M: IFF always inoperative in OFF mode.

P: Suspected crack in windshield.
M: Suspect you're right.

P: Number 3 engine missing.
M: Number 3 engine found on right wing after brief search.

P: Aircraft handles funny.
M: Aircraft warned to straighten up, fly right and be serious.

P: Mouse in cockpit.
M: Cat installed.

P: Noise coming from under instrument panel. Sounds like a midget pounding on something with a hammer.
M: Took hammer away from midget.

P: Target radar hums.
M: Reprogrammed target radar with lyrics.

Getting it right

Every year is important but 2012 is especially so because that's when the Olympics come to Britain. For anyone who cares about our country, it's vital that our extra million or so visitors return home believing that they have enjoyed a very positive and worthwhile customer experience. We want them to become what Frederick Reichheld calls "active promoter" customers, actively recommending Britain to their friends, colleagues and relatives as a place where you can be guaranteed a warm, memorable and cost-effective welcome.

So our vision for the Institute of Customer Service has the pursuit of the customer experience at its heart. Your vision should do the same. It doesn't matter what business you're in – your prosperity, survival, growth and profitability depend on your ability to generate favourable experiences among your customers. Nor does it matter how you deliver your customer experience – whether you do so face-to-face or online, over the telephone or through one of the shopping channels. The ingredients of a meaningful customer experience remain the same wherever you are and however you come into contact with your customers to construct a relationship with them that will go beyond the first purchase transaction.

Selling your first product to a new customer is easy (relatively speaking) – the trick is to sell to that customer again and again and again. If you can, you've immediately saved yourself a lot of stupid and avoidable effort, because it's always between five and 15 times more time-consuming and costly to find a new customer than it is to keep the ones you've already got.

And, by the way, the concept of the customer experience is just as relevant for you if you're employed, whether in a directly customer-facing job or not. If you deal with (paying) customers every day, then you don't need me to tell you that you have customers. But if you work in a back-office, support, processing or administrative function, then it's

Stories about customers and customer service experiences

sometimes too easy to lose sight of the fact that you have customers too. Just like 'real' customers everywhere, your customers value the quality of the experience they get from you. Of course they want whatever you deliver to them to be accurate, timely, relevant, efficient and competent – but like customers everywhere, they'll like it even better if you deliver your services with enthusiasm, with a smile, with a willingness to go the extra mile and with a readiness to focus on continuous improvement. If you create some positive customer experiences around you – with your seniors, your colleagues, associates and so forth – then (like a company that creates positive customer experiences) you'll benefit in all sorts of ways: you'll earn better appraisals, better salary increases, better chances for promotion and more job security (handy if redundancies beckon). What's more – and this is not trivial at all – you'll feel better about yourself.

There are some common features of the customer experience that should deserve the attention of every business that hopes to secure a strong base of loyal and supportive customers. These common features apply to all types of business – large or small, manufacturing, the professions, utilities, public or private – and to all types of service delivery channel.

For example, ICS commissioned Professor Robert Johnston of Warwick Business School to examine the characteristics of five companies that are, by common consent, viewed as 'world-class' for their service excellence. What we wanted to show, if we could, was that world-class service experiences depend upon the presence of a similar framework of strategic, managerial and operational practices – so that other organisations, if aspiring to be world-class themselves, could learn from these benchmark businesses.

From Professor Johnston's case studies – featuring First Direct, Tesco, the RAC, Shangri-La Hotels and Singapore Airlines – we conclude that world-class customer service is more likely to occur when the organisation is *easy to do business with* which, in turn involves four routines:

1. **The business delivers what it promises** – in quantity, quality, timescale and against all other relevant parameters

2. **It provides a personal touch**

– by treating the customer as an individual and also by providing named contacts within the company

3. **It goes the extra mile if it has to** – unconstrained by adherence to procedures or the imminence of a shift change

4. **It resolves problems well** – quickly, graciously and generously.

None of this is rocket science. (Very little ever is rocket science, except rocket science.) Yet it's amazing that only about 8% of businesses can authentically be described as 'world-class' in terms of the quality of the service experience they supply to their customers (and which their customers perceive to be truly exceptional).

What do these 8% of 'world-class' service businesses actually do? The answer is, essentially, three things:

1. **They design the right offers and experiences for the right customers.** They don't treat all their customers alike because they realise that different customers may want different things, like different levels of service, response times and so forth. In supermarkets, for example, it's now quite common for customers to be greeted by name at the checkout (assuming they have handed over their credit card early in the transaction) and although most customers welcome this more personalised approach, there is a significant minority that regards it as intrusive

2. **They deliver these propositions by focusing the entire organisation on them, especially with cross-functional collaboration.** These 'world-class' operators preach a single message – a 'big idea' – about the supremacy of the customer, and don't allow it to be diluted or compromised by anyone

3. **They develop their capabilities – creating new customer experiences through constant renewal.** They remain one step ahead of the customer, not one step behind. I call this the 'Tetley Teabag Tactic' because nobody knew they wanted round teabags until Tetley suddenly produced them – just as nobody knew they wanted satellite navigation, disposable nappies, power steering or mobile telephony until these products hit the streets. The world's best service businesses try to anticipate what the customer is going to want next because they

Stories about customers and customer service experiences

realise that if you mean what you say when you describe yourself as 'customer-led', you're never going to be higher than number two in the marketplace.

Deliberately seeking to create world-class service experiences for your customers is worth the effort for a number of very good reasons. First, a 'very satisfied' customer is six times more likely to buy again from you than a customer who is only 'satisfied' and for most organisations the attrition rates for dissatisfied customers are no different to those for the 'rationally satisfied'.

Second, your business may itself be dealing with customers who have personally enjoyed world-class customer experiences. This means that their expectations have been finely tuned and if you fail to meet them you can find that they take their future orders elsewhere.

Third, if you don't occupy a world-class slot, someone else will eventually see an opportunity, seize it and your business will begin to dissolve. This is exactly what happened to the retail banking field in 1994 when First Direct burst on the scene: the first bank to take service seriously, the first bank to treat its customers as equals, the first bank to ask customers what they wanted from a bank and then provide it. Now, more than 80% of First Direct's customers act as the bank's own marketing department and First Direct does virtually no advertising at all.

Fourth, the goal is emphatically not to produce customer satisfaction. Many businesses continue to spend lots of money trying to find out whether their customers are 'satisfied' and become very excited when they find that they are. Yet the reality is that customers nowadays *expect* to be satisfied, so will not become loyal merely because they are. To put it another way, customer 'satisfaction' and customer 'delight' are two entirely different things and it is only customer 'delight' that makes the difference.

In this chapter you can read about some of the customer experiences that help to bring lasting success, growth and profitability – everything, in fact, that you would want for yourself and your business.

... And here's another illustration of being a winner and a loser at the same time:

A friend recalls visiting a restaurant chain where the staff made her daughter's birthday particularly enjoyable. She thanked the manager who asked her to write to his boss - which she did.

A standard letter came back from the complaints department saying: "We are sorry to hear about your unfortunate experience but we will look into it and make sure it doesn't happen again".

The Daily Telegraph

The Physical and Emotional Mix of the Customer Experience

"There is definitely an emotional side to the customer experience.

The empathy that a Customer Service Advisor has with a customer is an example of emotional delivery.

The accuracy and consistency of the Customer Service Advisor is an example of the physical."

Peter Scott, Customer Services Director, T-Mobile

Roger Dow, a senior Vice-President at Marriott Hotels, asked his IT staff to come up with something that would give them a fraction of the 'customer recognition' capacity of the Ritz-Carlton Hotels – just enough to enable a clerk at the check-in desk to say "Welcome back" to a guest because the computer tells them that the guest has stayed there before.

The IT team came back a few weeks later and said they could do it for $1.3 million and it would take 18 months. Dow went ballistic.

Shortly after, he was visiting a small mid-western Marriott. As he approached the check-in desk, the clerk smiled warmly. "Welcome back sir," she said.

Dow dropped his bag with astonishment. "What did you say? I've been trying to get our IT people to make that work for months. Do you know who I am? I'm the VP of Marketing. I didn't tell you I'd been here before! It can't say that on the computer system," he blustered.

The check-in clerk, feeling she had done wrong, explained: "Well, you see, when the bellboy picks up the luggage from the car, he says to the guest: 'Is this your first visit?' You must have said 'No' and forgotten. Because, when he puts the bag down next to the desk here he winks at me. That's code. It means you're a returning guest, so I say: 'Welcome back sir'".

Told by customer service guru Don Peppers at the 2001 European Conference on Customer Management

Employee of the month is a good example of how somebody can be both a winner and a loser at the same time.

Demetri Martin

What a brave new world we live in:

"I believe the new trends include the requirement that the vehicle will work."

Sir Graham Day former Chief Executive, British Leyland

The message from Burger King:

"We may be the King, but you, my friend, are the almighty ruler."

Sharing knowledge with customers can make a big difference to the bottom line. A good example is provided by United Parcel Services (UPS), a company that has always assumed that on-time delivery was the primary concern of its customers. As a result, the cornerstone of its quality policy was guaranteed next-day delivery for all packages. In the mid-1990s everything that the company did was geared around a service quality which aimed to deliver every package by 10.30 on the morning following collection. The times taken to call a lift, the delay in answering doorbells, were all taken into account in producing precise schedules. The company even shaved corners off its delivery drivers' seats to speed their entry and exit from their delivery vans.

Having assumed that delivery time was critical, the company then set up a series of internal measures to monitor the reliability of its delivery performance. It simply assumed that if it met these targets customers would perceive it as offering high quality. Of course, customers were very happy with this reliability and service standard, but when UPS management broadened the questions on its customer surveys, managers received a big surprise. They found that customers valued an opportunity to chat with delivery drivers to get practical tips and advice on how to package and ship parcels. A driver that shot in and out of a delivery like lightning to meet a tight performance target didn't have time to share any knowledge.

As a response, the company created a 13-minute space in each driver's day to allow the driver to chat with customers. When it was introduced, this time allowance cost UPS $4 million in drivers' time each year, but the company reckons that the additional sales achieved are many times higher.

CUSTOMER CARE:

This succulent sun-ripened fruit is ready to fill you with a burst of intense flavours to savour. And if for any reason it doesn't, please let us know and we will try to win you over forever.

Message on the wrapper for Whitworths 'Frootz' (dried fruits)

Commitment is doing something with the same level of enthusiasm as you displayed when you said you would do it.

Don Peppers

The factory of the future will have only two employees: a man and a dog.

The man will be there to feed the dog.

The dog will be there to keep the man from touching the equipment.

Warren Bennis

Unless you take pains to provide the best possible service, and do so at a competitive market price (i.e. salary), you'll find it hard to keep customers. They'll replace you with a better service provider. In essence, somebody else will 'steal your business'.

The more you allow your service to go soft, the greater the odds you could end up in some downsizing statistics. Or, the organisation might simply decide to outsource your work, to farm it out to some other firm that specialises in doing what you do.

You must get close – intimately close – to your customers. Seek regular, direct contact with them. Build a strong relationship. Deliver the highest quality service possible. Anticipate their needs and develop a reputation for responsiveness.

In the final analysis, customers are your only source of job security.

Quotations from The Employee Handbook of New Work Habits for a Radically Changing World by Price Pritchett & Associates Inc, 1994

This is a people business ...

"No more missions or visions," proclaims a card on Henry Engelhardt's desk. "Our motto is to have fun, satisfy customers and make money."

Engelhardt is Chief Executive of the Admiral Group of insurance businesses based in Cardiff.

Engelhardt doesn't wear a suit. "We don't have a dress code," he says. "We want our people to express their personalities on the phone. If we forced them to dress a certain way, maybe we'd be inhibiting their personalities as well. We work very hard to ensure that people like what they do here. It has to do with entertainment, quizzes, shopping trips, Alton Towers and Christmas parties. It has to do with communication, it has to do with the idea of staff trust, of sharing.

"This is a people business. There are people like our people at other firms dotted around this country doing very similar jobs and in the end the customer is buying the person on the end of the phone. When you get on the phone with someone, you can hear whether that person is happy. It gives a better feeling about the company if they are.

"We had a customer write in 1995 saying, 'I have been a customer for 20 years'. Astonishing, really, given that Admiral only started up in 1993."

The Empty Chair at Amazon ...

"You stretch the edges of your market by working your customer interface with an intensity you have never done before, listening and inventing for customers simultaneously."

At Amazon they do this through:

- Simplicity and elegance
- Consistency and weekly vigilance – "Monthly or quarterly monitoring of what customers are saying is ridiculous today. Weekly knowledge of what your customers are saying is the minimum you can get away with"
- Process innovation
- A belief that the customer experience is more important than short-term profits
- The Empty Chair – "It's our first staff meeting at Amazon. Twelve of us are crammed into a stuffy room. Yet, as the room fills up, Jeff (Bezos) keeps his hand on the seat of the chair next to him so no-one can sit there. There we are, jammed together and this seat is kept empty. As he starts the meeting Jeff says: 'I'm keeping this seat empty for the customer. Everything we talk about in this meeting over the next hour has to be about the customer'."

At Domino Pizza each order is only worth $15. Yet they calculated that a regular customer over 10 years is worth $5,000. Calculating this figure led to a significant change in attitudes ... every delivery person learned to feel he or she was delivering to someone worth $5,000 ... the chefs felt they were making a pizza worth $5,000.

Robin Buchanan,
Bain International

The Wit and Wisdom of Jack Welch

When he reigned as the Chief Executive for General Electric, Jack Welsh grew its market value to more than $500 billion and became 'The World's Most Admired Business Leader'. These are a few of his contributions to the sum of human knowledge.

- What to measure
  - If I had to run a company on three measures, those measures would be customer satisfaction, employee satisfaction and cash flow

- Build confidence: that's your job description
  - If you're not simple, you can't be fast. And, if you're not fast, you're dead. So everything we do [at GE] focuses on building self-confidence in people so they can be simple

- Set your people free
  - You've got to balance freedom with some control, but you've got to have more freedom than you've ever dreamed of

- Shout when you win
  - People feel guilty about stopping to celebrate a little victory ... but it lets people know they've won. It's so critical to an institution. It brings it alive, gives it character

- Numbers aren't enough
  - Numbers aren't the vision. Numbers are the product. I never talk about numbers

- Fair doesn't mean 'the same'
  - Every person should be treated fairly in an organisation, but every person should be treated differently in an organisation

- Meet customers more often
  - Welch made a point of personally meeting GE's major customers in spring and autumn each year. He put much of his and GE's customer insights down to these twice-a-year reality checks with customers.

The 'secret' of First Direct

First Direct, from a standing start in 1994, is now the UK's most recommended bank with customer satisfaction second to none. Over 80% of First Direct's customers are 'active promoters' for the bank – which means that they say good things about it and recommend it to their friends, colleagues, relatives and other associates – compared with 17% for all the other banks put together.

How has First Direct done it? Well, the first thing they did, when they were setting themselves up, was to ask a sample of potential customers what they would like from a bank. Incredibly, nobody had done this before.

The results from this survey indicated that bank customers want, above all, five things:

1. Make it easy for me
2. Leave me in control
3. Know me as an individual
4. Treat me as an equal
5. Give me confidence.

The second thing that First Direct did was to realise that if they were to satisfy these five needs for their customers, then they had to satisfy the same five needs for their staff as well. Above all, they had to:

- Develop processes designed around the experience and aspirations of the customer

- Recruit, select, train and develop people with the requisite self-confidence and 'will' to perform in line with First Direct's customer-centric values.

What First Direct found through bitter experience, moreover, was that people who have previously worked in financial services don't fit in with First Direct's culture. This is because the approach used by other financial service businesses is so out of step with the philosophy adopted at First Direct.

So First Direct's 'secret' isn't really a secret at all. They have been entirely open about what they were trying to do and how they were going to do it. What is fascinating is why so few other organisations – especially in retail banking, but not necessarily confined to banking – have followed directly in First Direct's pioneering footsteps.

> The real opportunity is not from understanding customer satisfaction, but customer preference. Satisfied customers still leave you because they find an experience they prefer elsewhere. You need an experience preference model, not a customer satisfaction model.
>
> *Lou Carbone, CEO, Experience Engineering Inc*

Sometimes rocket scientists do know something about customer service.

Scientists at NASA built a gun specifically to launch dead chickens at the windshields of airlines, military jets and the space shuttle, all travelling at maximum velocity. The idea was to simulate the frequent incidents of collisions with airborne fowl to test the strength of the windshields.

British engineers heard about the gun and were eager to test it on the windshields of their new high-speed trains.

Arrangements were made and a gun was sent over to Britain.

When the gun was fired, the engineers stood shocked as the chicken hurtled out of the barrel, crashed into the shatterproof shield, smashed it to smithereens, blasted through the control console, snapped the driver's backrest in two and embedded itself in the back wall of the cabin, like an arrow shot from a bow.

The horrified Brits sent NASA information about these disastrous results, along with designs of the windshield, and begged the US scientists for suggestions.

NASA responded with a one-line message:

"Defrost the chicken."

Stories about customers and customer service experiences

Do you provide world-class service to your customers?

Test yourself against these questions:

- I know who my customers are
- The quality of the service I give to my customers is my highest priority, above all else
- I make sure my customers trust me
- I prioritise my service tasks around the needs of my customers
- I'm always willing to 'go the extra mile' for my customers
- I work hard to create long-term relationships with my customers
- In dealing with my customers I am unfailingly polite, considerate, tolerant and friendly
- I'm always trying to think of ways to improve my service performance
- My customers always know what to expect from me
- I keep my customers well informed at all times
- My customers have absolute confidence in what I do for them
- I am always available for my customers.

> The only difference between a creative and a non-creative person is that creatives tend not to have a voice in their head saying, "That's not going to work. That's a stupid idea".
>
> Peter Molyneux, computer game developer

> A leader takes people where they want to go. A great leader takes people where they don't necessarily want to go, but ought to be.
>
> Rosalynn Carter

> I have only empowered my people to say 'yes' to a customer. If they want to say 'no', they have to talk to a manager and clear it with them first.
>
> Jan Carlzon during his time as President and Chief Executive Officer at Scandinavian Airline Systems

ICS is the professional body for customer service. We are a membership organisation with a community of over 350 organisational members and nearly 8,000 individual members. Our mission is to lead customer service performance and professionalism with the aim of being the authoritative voice of customer service – the touchstone for those whose focus is on the delivery of world-class service experiences.

The Institute's core aims are to:

- recruit and retain a broad-based and significant organisational membership drawn from the private, public and third sectors and provide opportunities for members to learn from each other

- promote customer service professionalism; define customer service skills, set professional standards and support individuals in achieving them; and build individual membership, providing professional recognition and support for continuing development

- work in partnership with our members and others, such as business schools, to develop and continually update knowledge and expertise about customer service and the delivery of world-class service experiences Promote learning based on this knowledge and expertise, for example, through a knowledge bank, research reports, publications, models, conferences and other events

- develop services and products to help, primarily, our members transform and sustain the quality and reputation of their service delivery

- influence those whose decisions impact on the importance attached to customer service and the way in which it is delivered, for example, politicians, regulators, directors, senior managers and, of course, customers

- recognise, promote and celebrate the success of organisations and individuals in achieving customer service excellence

- organise ourselves and work in a way that ensures our own customers enjoy world-class service experiences.

To find out more about membership and ICS activities – from Breakthrough Research to customer satisfaction to individual development programmes, etc – visit our website: **instituteofcustomerservice.com** or email: **enquiries@icsmail.co.uk** or call: 01206 571716.